THE FUTURE OF CLASSIFICATION

The Future of Classification

edited by

Rita Marcella and Arthur Maltby

ASHGATE

© Rita Marcella and Arthur Maltby 2000

All rights reserved. No part of this publication may be
reproduced, stored in a retrieval system, or transmitted in any
form or by any means, electronic, mechanical, photocopying,
recording or otherwise without the permission of the publisher.

Published by
Gower Publishing Limited
Gower House
Croft Road
Aldershot
Hampshire GU11 3HR
England

Ashgate Publishing Company
Suite 420
101 Cherry Street
Burlington, VT 05401-4405
USA

British Library Cataloguing in Publication Data
The future of classification
  1. Classification – Books
  I. Marcella, Rita   II. Maltby, Arthur
  025.4'2

ISBN 0 566 07992 5

Library of Congress Cataloging-in-Publication Data

The future of classification / edited by Rita Marcella and Arthur Maltby.
    p. cm.
  Includes bibliographical references and index.
  ISBN 0-566-07992-5 (hardback)
  1. Classification—Books.   I. Marcella, Rita.   II. Maltby, Arthur.

Z696.A4 F88 2000
025.4'2—dc21
                                                              99–046030

Reprinted 2002, 2005

Phototypeset in 10 point Palatino by Intype London Ltd
and printed in Great Britain by Antony Rowe Ltd, Chippenham, Wiltshire

Contents

Notes on contributors vii

Introduction xi
Rita Marcella and Arthur Maltby

1 **Do we still need classification?** 1
 Eric Hunter

2 **Organizing knowledge: the need for system and unity** 19
 Arthur Maltby and Rita Marcella

3 **Can classification yield an evaluative principle for information retrieval?** 33
 Julian Warner

4 **Information technology and new directions** 43
 Robert Newton

5 **Classification and the Internet** 59
 Alan MacLennan

6 **The future of faceted classification** 69
 A. C. Foskett

7 **The Dewey Decimal Classification in the twenty-first century** 81
 Joan S. Mitchell

8 **UDC in the twenty-first century** 93
 I. C. McIlwaine

9	The Library of Congress Classification *Lois Mai Chan and Theodora L. Hodges*	105
10	Sources for investigating the development of bibliographic classification *M. P. Satija*	129

Index 141

Notes on contributors

Lois Mai Chan
Professor, School of Library and Information Science, University of Kentucky, Lexington, KY, Lois Mai Chan is the author of several books on knowledge organization, including *Cataloging and Classification*, *Dewey Decimal Classification: A Practical Guide*, *Immroth's Guide to the Library of Congress Classification*, *Library of Congress Subject Headings: Principles and Application*, and *Thesauri Used in Online Databases*. From 1986 to 1991, she served as the chair of the Decimal Classification Editorial Policy Committee. Her research interests include classification, controlled vocabulary, authority control, metadata, and online retrieval.

A. C. Foskett
After working in public and special libraries, A. C. Foskett started teaching full-time at Loughborough in 1961. In 1966 he moved to the College of Librarianship Wales, and in 1973 he took charge of the new library school at the South Australian Institute of Technology. He retired at the end of 1991 as Professor of Library and Information Management. He has been interested in classification all his working life, and is probably best known as the author of the textbook *The Subject Approach to Information*, of which the 5th edition was published in 1996.

Theodora L. Hodges
Formerly on the faculty of the School of Library and Information Studies (now School of Information Management and Systems), University of California, Berkeley, Theodora L. Hodges is co-author of 'Subject Cataloguing and Classification', in *Technical Services Today and Tomorrow*, 2nd edn, Michael Gorman, ed. (Englewood, CO: Libraries Unlimited, 1998). Her areas of specialization are cataloguing and indexing.

Eric Hunter
Eric Hunter is Emeritus Professor of Information Management, Liverpool John Moores University. He retired as Head of Information Management, Liverpool Business School in 1995. He has written and researched widely in education, librarianship and information handling. Monographic publications include: *ABC of BASIC: an introduction to programming for librarians* (1982); *Cataloguing* (with K. G. B. Bakewell) (3rd edn 1991); *Computerised Cataloguing* (1985); *Examples Illustrating AACR2* (with Margaret Graham), (1994); *Introduction to AACR2: a programmed guide* (1989). His works have been translated into various languages including Catalan, Chinese and Japanese.

Alan MacLennan
Alan MacLennan is a lecturer at the School of Information and Media, and the Course Leader for the Postgraduate Diploma/MSc in Electronic Information Management, specializing in the teaching of information retrieval and information technology. His research interests include programming, the Internet and the retrieval of fiction.

Arthur Maltby
Arthur Maltby worked in public, academic and industrial libraries before becoming a lecturer, a Head of Department of Information Studies, and finally a government adviser on education and libraries. He is the author of books and papers on various topics including Irish history and bibliography, information retrieval systems and adult learning opportunities. Now retired, his current activities include writing under the pseudonym A. M. Challinor, on Shakespeare and twentieth-century Shakespearean commentators.

Rita Marcella
Rita Marcella is the Deputy Head, School of Information and Media, the Robert Gordon University. As a Reader, she has been involved in a number of funded research projects in areas such as citizenship information, the information needs of rural business, European information policy and help-desk management. Prior monographs include: *A New Manual of Classification* (with Robert Newton) (1994); and *Biography and Children* (with Stuart Hannabuss) (1992). She has worked as a classifier/cataloguer in a university library.

I. C. McIlwaine
I. C. McIlwaine is Professor of Library and Information Studies in the University of London (formerly Reader in Classification and Indexing in the University of London), Director of the School of Library, Archive and

Information Studies, University College London since 1995 (formerly Departmental Tutor). She has also been Editor-in-Chief of the Universal Decimal Classification since 1993, Chairman of FID/CR since 1997, a Member of the IFLA Committee on Classification and Indexing since 1995 and Chairman since 1997.

Joan S. Mitchell

Joan S. Mitchell is Editor-in-Chief of the Dewey Decimal Classification and Executive Director of OCLC Forest Press. She served as a member of the Decimal Classification Editorial Policy Committee 1985–93, and chaired the committee from 1992 to 1993. Currently Chair of the Permanent UNIMARC Committee Working Group on a Classification Format, she also serves on the editorial board of *Knowledge Organization* and is a member of the Scientific Advisory Council of ISKO. Prior to becoming Dewey Editor, she was Director of Educational Technology at Carnegie Mellon University and an adjunct professor in the School of Library and Information Sciences at the University of Pittsburgh. She has written and spoken extensively on knowledge organization and subject analysis.

Robert Newton

Robert Newton is a Senior Lecturer at the School of Information and Media at the Robert Gordon University. He has been involved in funded research projects looking at strategic development of the Internet and its use both in higher education teaching and in public libraries. He previously collaborated with Rita Marcella on *A New Manual of Classification*. His previous employment includes working as a cataloguer at the Welsh National School of Medicine and as a library systems analyst with SLS Ltd. He currently teaches and researches in the fields of information retrieval and information and communication technologies.

M. P. Satija

Dr M. P. Satija has been in the library profession for the last 25 years. He has authored 20 books, as well as many articles and book reviews; and has contributed papers for several national and international conferences. He is the Indian coordinator of the International Society for Knowledge Organization (ISKO), Denmark, and is associated with many library journals. At present he is a Reader in the Department of Library and Information Science, Guru Nanak Dev University, Amritsar.

Julian Warner

Julian Warner is Assistant Director – Research, School of Management, The Queen's University of Belfast and has worked as a faculty member in information studies at The Queen's University of Belfast since 1984. Previously he was a student at the universities of Newcastle, Oxford and Sheffield as well as a research assistant in glass production and a trainee at York University Library.

Introduction
Rita Marcella and Arthur Maltby

The purpose of this book is to bring together specialist views on the way ahead for that perennial activity, or old workhorse, we call classification. It is now almost thirty years since one of us edited what was a pioneer attempt to bring together such an international collection of perspectives and prophecies.[1] He was fortunate then, as we both are now, in the calibre of the contributors. The start of a fresh millennium seems a particularly appropriate time to look anew at trends and the prospects for major systems. Our specialist writers, drawn from four continents, show the persistence of some long-standing issues and identify new ones.

Retrospect and prospect

However, we should first glance back. When that 1972 volume was published, the last of the great general classification makers, Ranganathan, reviewed and welcomed the volume warmly, in what was almost certainly his final contribution to professional literature. Understandably, all the contributors who were advocates for a particular system of classification predicted a sound future for it. And yet, apart from a highly optimistic prophecy by Mills that the new Bliss Bibliographic Classification would be completed in the 1970s and perhaps some excessive optimism concerning the future of The Colon Classification, there was nothing said that proved conspicuously inaccurate. Bob Freeman's dream scenario of a virtual reality situation apparently matching classification with each individual user's immediate needs was ahead of its time, but is now surely very significant. It is also pleasing, in this new work, to see tribute paid to the enduring quality of the ideas on the UDC discussed by the late Geoffrey Lloyd in the 1972 collection, cited above.

What of the situation now in comparison with the state of affairs then? We still could not get an international 'philosophy of classification', agreed upon in all aspects, even if we wanted one. Yet systems and speculations not only survive, but flourish. Classification endures – not only explicitly in the great systems, but also implicitly as a mode of thinking crucial in the storage and retrieval of knowledge.

There is naturally a legacy involved in all classifying: in some respects that inheritance inspires and sustains, in others it haunts us – one cannot, in the interests of modernity, change call marks on a vast existing physical collection (or its records) overnight. Thus, of the old issues that remain, a notable one is the problem of moving with the times while maintaining stability of structure within a system. One of the new challenges on the demand side of the equation is that there is need to take account of changes in society which may affect patterns of knowledge exploration – both the amount and strategy of information seeking. The customer is (or should be) still monarch. One factor on the supply side is that there is more 'grey' or fringe material, existing as quasi-publications, to consider. Another, of course, is new technology opportunities.

Questioning and affirmations

The contributions which follow cover many themes and opinions. Eric Hunter has long striven to make the understanding of this subject easier. In Chapter 1, with characteristic humour and clarity, he shows, with telling examples, the pervasive nature and enduring uses of the classificatory activity. While so doing, Hunter notes that some writers, either anxious to import new skills into the professional curriculum or simply to 'downsize' the contribution of older ones, have queried the continuing value of studying cataloguing and classification. He provides a robust retort to this 'classification is no longer significant' school of thought. Chapter 2, by the editors, is also of a relatively introductory nature. It emphasizes both the value of saving enquirers' time and the need to gather the most relevant information in a world where 'information choice' is ever increasing. This chapter also makes a plea for more conscious planning in information management strategies, so that classification is complemented appropriately by other tools or resources.

The third chapter, by Julian Warner, is much more 'advanced' in theme and tone. It shrewdly queries the long-held assumption in information retrieval systems that recall capacity on a named theme is, along with relevance testing, a reliable measure of effectiveness. Meeting users' needs may be an art; it is certainly not an exact science. An enquirer may have difficulty in fully grasping or articulating requirements. Warner's chapter claims that conventional retrieval theory has been too restrictive, trying to span, by artificial means, something which may be essentially fluid. One is perhaps reminded, in this, of the limitations of management 'performance indicators'; these seek to 'measure' achievement, but are necessarily imperfect instruments since we are concerned with quality rather than quantity – and quality does not lend itself to precise measurement Be that as it may, Warner thinks rigid prescriptions of what constitutes recall and relevance may well have imposed barriers, thus divorcing information retrieval theory from actual day-to-day practice. He looks to classification, or its equivalents, to provide a wider imaginative stimulus – what he chooses to call 'exploratory capacity' or 'informed choice'.

Technologically driven impetus

The last idea is one which might be particularly helpful in the context of modern technology, where our main focus comes from Chapter 4 (Robert Newton) and Chapter 5 (Alan MacLennan). This factor, which Immanuel Kant might well have called 'the technological imperative', is undoubtedly the biggest supply challenge. Responding to computer-linked opportunities most appropriately can make classification and other retrieval tools varied and fluid, by drawing to the full on advantageous methods of retrieval hitherto denied or unsuspected. Possibilities include the intelligent computer sometimes anticipating the needs of an information seeker by initiating the provision of extra potentially useful information on screen. So Chapters 4 and 5 give us perspectives on digital libraries, and automatic classification, along with the potential and problems of the Internet. And technology has a different kind of input to offer via help to the editors of large classification schemes, where it can provide a fillip or elixir for schedule and index revision.

Principles and systems

In Chapter 6, Tony Foskett illustrates the idea of dividing a subject into its constituent parts and providing rules for the assembly of the symbols which represent these. It is shown that this principle of facet analysis, under whatever name and however imperfectly recognized, has been with library classification systems from the very beginning. His examples span many schemes: the key message is that sound principles of thoroughgoing subject analysis have a lasting place in organizing knowledge. Foskett also, discussing aspects of his paper via correspondence with one of the editors, points out that citation order is crucial for a physical display, where it seeks to reflect majority needs, but is much less so in machine-based searching. This point does not invalidate the theory. However, it does mean that many more permutations can be allowed. Thus minority interest groupings, as well as majority ones, can be reflected in the total display of subject associations.

Joan Mitchell must be well aware that a system with the strengths and success of the Dewey Decimal Classification (DDC) could rest on its laurels, but the message of Chapter 7 is one of vision and ambition. To be at the helm of an enterprise and be asked to contribute a specialist chapter on it may be a mixed blessing: the very closeness may inhibit forecasts for the future. So perhaps the editors of this book should insist here that the future for DDC is extremely secure, despite the criticism (inevitable in such a widely used system) made over the years. In concluding, Mitchell echoes very briefly a point made in different ways by other contributors – the need to educate a new breed of information technologists about the continuing value of established retrieval principles. Some of our specialist contributors are more sanguine about the prospects of this than are others. Certainly, looking in any typical computing reference work (such as the example here cited),[2] under the stem 'Class . . .', suggests no immediate grounds for optimism.

Professor I. C. McIlwaine, in Chapter 8, shows how the UDC has changed and is changing. It too has many problems to face, not least coping with the diversity of the contexts in which it is applied and in facing up to demands upon it without alienating established users. It too copes well. This reminds us that particularly noticeable in Chapters 7 to 9 is the strong spirit of cooperation between the big three general systems: the war, if ever there was one, is over.

Chapter 9, by Chan and Hodges, shows just how active the Library of Congress Classification (LCC) team has been in recent years, and how opportunities have been well grasped to rejuvenate the system and maximize its adaptability. It too can face the future with confidence. Mention of this chapter reminds us that our contributors write without constraint other than that of length: they need not always fully agree. Thus it is that when the authors of this chapter quote Gerry McKiernan on a technological application of LCC, they do so with understandable enthusiasm, but Newton's view of this matter in Chapter 4 is not so approving. These varying perspectives make for healthy debate among students, as they do among the specialists.

Envoi

India has a special place in the development of library classification, and M. P. Satija's analysis of classification literature in the final chapter is by way of celebrating the maturity of the subject and its emancipation from the restrictions so evident in the early attempts to develop a distinctive theory for it. But celebration does not mean relaxation: some of us find all matters classificatory a fascinating theme, but judgement must always be by practical achievement – the contribution that classification, both in its explicit and implicit forms, makes to a good information service or knowledge store. That, in a world of rapid change, is the ever-present challenge.

This introduction was naturally the last part of this book to be completed. Looking at the chapters again, we note that some predictions are inevitably made. These rest in the hands of time. They may not prove correct in all details; this does not make them any the less intriguing. And in some cases, chapters, as first received by us, have overlapped a little; however, we have allowed a theme to crop up in more than one chapter if a distinctive point or perspective is involved.

It has been a pleasure to invite and edit this new collection of papers. These writers, taken together, have much useful factual information to impart, along with thought-provoking ideas based on a wealth of experience. We are most grateful to them. We would also seize this opportunity to express thanks to four other individuals: Elizabeth Davidson and Graeme Baxter at the Robert Gordon University for unflagging secretarial and administrative support, Suzie Duke, our Commissioning Editor, and at Gower, Elizabeth Teague, copy-editor, for her valued advice and hard work.

Notes

1 A. Maltby (ed.) (1972), *Classification in the 1970s*, London: Bingley.
2 *Dictionary of Computing*, 4th edn, Oxford: University Press, 1996.

1 Do we still need classification?
Eric Hunter

Classification is basic to life

My wife is a great fan of Harrison Ford; although pseudo-intellectual snobbery prevents me from admitting it to her, I suppose that I am too. We thoroughly enjoy many of the films in which he stars. As I write, several, including *Working Girl* and *The Fugitive*, are being shown on television. Barry Norman, in the *Radio Times*, reminds us, however, that we might well have been denied the pleasure that Ford gives us, for in the early seventies Ford became seriously dissatisfied with the sameness and blandness of the work that he was being offered so he gave up acting and became a carpenter instead (Norman, 1997). In point of fact, he became a very good carpenter and examples of his work are to be found to this day in many a home in Beverly Hills (ibid.).

What has all this got to do with classification? When Ford was whittling wood, he kept all his carpentry tools laid out in order of type and size right through his entire workshop (Courtenay, 1994). He realized that this would make his work that much easier. Apparently Ford even keeps his shirts and socks in colour-coded rows (ibid.). Clearly, he recognizes that 'classification lies at the base of every well-managed life and occupation' (Maltby, 1975, p. 15).

As the above examples show, in essence classification simply means the grouping together of like things according to common qualities or characteristics. This automatically implies the separation of the unlike. By putting all of his *cutting* tools together, Ford would immediately separate them from his *drilling* tools and from his *smoothing* tools. But the issue of classification is far more important than whether Ford could locate easily the right tool or the right pair of socks; classification not only makes things easier to find; it is basic to our very existence. As human beings, we are able to recognize a member of a particular class because it displays certain characteristics common to that class but not to others. Consider the following collection:

From observation one is able immediately to group together like entities:

It is essential for a person to be able to think logically in this way and to make such distinctions. Otherwise, perhaps, one would be keeping bananas as pets or waiting for cats to grow on trees! Send for the men in white coats!

Imagine how difficult and time-consuming the arrangement shown below would make shopping in your local supermarket. It would be *chaos*!

Wine	Lamb	Bread	
	Potatoes	Beer	Tea
	Cakes	Beef	Butter	Cabbage
	Margarine	Spirits	Pies	Coffee
	Cocoa	Pork	Carrots	
Chicken	Beans	Cheese	Liqueurs

Classification makes things much easier!

Lamb	Bread	Wine	Potatoes	Tea	Butter
Beef	Cakes	Beer	Carrots	Coffee	Margarine
Pork	Pies	Spirits	Beans	Cocoa	Cheese
Chicken		Liqueurs	Cabbage		

If classification is basic to our very existence, so fundamental in our lives, can the humble librarian and information worker afford to ignore it? The answer is a resounding 'no'! Its value must continue to be recognized and it must be adopted to meet today's needs.

Classification in the library or information service

Shelf arrangement

When Harrison Ford gave up acting, 'He joined the local library to read up on carpentry and woodwork ... before proceeding to totally strip and gut his home from top to bottom ... and rebuild the entire house to his own specification' (Sellers, 1993, p. 33). When first he was shown where the carpentry books were located on the library shelves, he found them nestling amongst other works which might also be of use to him – books on bricklaying, plastering, plumbing and so on. These related subjects had been brought together by means of *classification*.

This is the first major use of classification in libraries and information services, and what a vital use it is – the systematic organization, by subject, of books and other materials on the shelves. Starting from ancient times, there have been many attempts to devise suitable schemes, both general and special.

Even a very broad subject grouping, one which does not attempt to adhere to a detailed scheme, can still be looked upon as 'classification', that is, as the 'bringing together of like and the separation of unlike'. A number of libraries have adopted such an approach for shelf arrangement, and some have made use of so-called 'reader interest' categories such as 'Do it yourself'. However, the major example of a broad subject arrangement, where collections of books are concerned, is most probably the bookshop. Here books are usually arranged in general sections such as 'languages', 'education', 'history', 'business' and 'travel'. How many of we readers though, I wonder, have been frustrated at times by such an arrangement? Whilst it might be adequate for general browsing, although even this is doubtful, if one is searching for a specific subject one can be forced to scan shelf after shelf after shelf. The bookshops themselves have realized the impracticality of this in certain instances; witness the breakdown of the 'Computer' section into 'General works', 'Operating systems', 'Windows', 'Programming languages', 'Packages', 'The Internet', and so on. 'Programming languages' might be divided further into 'C', 'Pascal', 'Visual Basic', and so on; and 'Packages' into 'Database management', 'Desktop publishing', 'Spreadsheets', 'Word processing', and so on. This is, to this present author, a very clear admission that classification is the only answer.

'Classification, then,' Maltby tells us, 'is a tool for very simple but infinitely important purposes. Its whole object is to secure an order which will be useful to readers and to those who seek information with the smallest complication of search or other effort. It is a technique designed to expedite the full use of the knowledge stored in books and other material housed in the collection' (Maltby, 1975).

Searching

The last sentence in the paragraph above indicates that, aside from the organization and location of the materials on the shelves, classification has a further essential part to play – assisting in the search process.

Imagine that you are on duty as a library assistant one day when you are approached by a reader and presented with the query: 'Have you anything on roses?' 'I believe so,' you reply politely. 'Just wait a moment, please.' You go to the shelves and there is nothing dealing specifically with roses.

What do you do? Being an efficient library assistant, you would, in all probability, look for something on flowers, or gardening, to see if there are any items that contain relevant information. By doing this, you have carried out a process of classification. You have identified the superordinate classes to which the required subject belongs.

The 'Roses' example is a simple one. Most people would know that roses are flowers which are grown in gardens. But what do you do if you do not know? Then you must find out. That is what the librarian or information worker's job is all about, not necessarily to *know* but to be able to *find out*! The query might be for a subject which you immediately recognize, for example 'Astronomy', or for something which is outside of one's knowledge at the given time, for example 'Kepler's laws'. If one did not recognize the latter topic, then one would clearly have to ascertain more information from the enquirer and consult the catalogue and perhaps other indexes and reference works. There are, of course, many such reference tools available.

The library catalogue

In a library, the 'key' to the shelf arrangement and a major tool for searching is the catalogue, a listing and essential guide to the library collection. Computerized library catalogues are now the norm, giving the user online access (OPAC – Online Public Access Catalogue). However, many researchers have concluded that the online catalogue, despite its numerous virtues, has not improved *subject* access. In this respect, some online catalogues offer nothing more than a 'keyword from title' facility, as illustrated in the following example of a catalogue search menu:

T	TITLE (keywords)
A	AUTHOR / EDITOR
O	ORGANIZATION
I	ISBN

Searching under keyword from title obviously requires the title words to reflect the subject clearly. Too often this does not happen; the titles *Exchanging to win in the endgame*, *The killer Grob* and *New ideas in the French defence*, although relevant, would not be retrieved if a search were made under the keyword 'Chess'. Such titles require 'enrichment' by the addition of appropriate subject terms.

One of the basic features which the traditional manual classified catalogue offers is the ability to look in an alphabetical subject index for the classification number for a particular subject and then to go to that number in a classified sequence to find relevant items. Not only is this an efficient way to find all the items dealing with a specific subject, but it also facilitates browsing for coordinate, subordinate and superordinate related subjects. Unfortunately, in some online catalogues, the only way to find the class number of a subject is to find the details relating to a specific item by searching for its author or title. Then, when the classified sequence is consulted, all that might be found is an indication of the number of occurrences, for example:

Your search: 001.6442		
1	001.6442 ALL	1
2	001.6442 AVI	1
3	001.6442 BAM	1
4	001.6442 BEN	2

This necessitates calling up each item, one by one, in order to ascertain which of them are of relevance, a tedious process and hardly an efficient search methodology.

This was the approach offered, until a year or two ago, by the Dynix system at Liverpool John Moores University. More recently a subject search facility has been introduced. Here, for example, are extracts from the result of a search for the subject 'Classification':

Your search: CLASSIFICATION		38 matches		
				Titles
1	025.43	–	U.D.C.: CLASSIFICATION: LIBRARIES	42
2	025.466	–	INDUSTRIAL CLASSIFICATION: CLASSIFICATION: LIBRARIES	5
3	550.12	–	GEOLOGY: CLASSIFICATION	1
...				
9	025.4	–	CLASSIFICATION: LIBRARIES	56
...				
11	616.890012	–	PSYCHIATRY: CLASSIFICATION	3
...				
21	112	–	CLASSIFICATION OF KNOWLEDGE: METAPHYSICS: PHILOSOPHY	3

Any of the numbers on the left above can be selected to see a list of the items at a particular class number. For example, selecting 3 would give the result:

MURRAY, J.W. A GUIDE TO CLASSIFICATION IN GEOLOGY

If 21 were selected, none of the three titles listed, for example *Derivation of rural housing profiles*, include the word classification and therefore would not be retrieved by a keyword from title search under that term.

The improvement that the introduction of this subject search facility has made in this university library is dramatic and demonstrates forcibly the value of using a classified approach to improve access. I am not arguing that the manual, classified catalogue approach should necessarily be *the* approach in an online catalogue. The computer has given us a wonderful, flexible capability which offers search possibilities that are impossible in a manual catalogue and we must make full use of all of these 'added value' facilities. What I am saying is that classification does not play any significant role in many OPACs and that the lessons learned over many years from classified catalogues and from classification research have not been incorporated in many online systems. It is not that the subject approach used in the classified catalogue is perfect – far from it, there are numerous difficulties – but it is patently clear that the use of other subject approaches in OPACs has not led to any improvement. Indeed, in some cases subject retrieval is far worse. Despite the problems, I would contend that to ignore classificatory techniques is to ignore one of the most powerful access tools that we possess.

In North America, research into the role of classification in searching and the practical use of classification in catalogues has been much less marked than in the rest of the world. 'The present situation in America is one in which infrequent articles on classification theory appear in obscure journals or conference reports' (Quinn, 1994). The American 'call number', which consists of the classification number with additions to identify the individual book, is most often used to indicate a specific shelf location, a 'mark and park' device: the 'use of classification in American libraries serves the limited purpose of physical placement on shelves' (Huestis, 1988).

The United States has always preferred the alphabetical approach to cataloguing and indexing and a 'dictionary'-type arrangement where authors, titles and subjects are listed in one alphabetical sequence. What has often been ignored, however, is that for an alphabetical subject approach to be successful, it must be based on classification.

The advantages of relating a classificatory element to alphabetical indexing can be clearly demonstrated. Examine the following list of terms:

AIR SPORTS	CHEMISTRY
ARCHAEOLOGY	DENTISTRY
BOATING	GEOGRAPHY
BOTANY	HISTORY

LITHOGRAPHY   SWIMMING
RELIGION   TEACHING
SAILING   WATER SPORTS
SPANISH   WATERSKIING
SPORTS   WELDING
STATISTICS   WINDSURFING

This is only a very brief alphabetical list but it illustrates how related terms can be swamped and the relationship between them lost amongst many, many other unrelated terms. Clearly, references linking related terms are required, for example: 'SPORTS *see also* Air sports; Water sports'. Interspersed with other entries, such a listing can become far more complex than its apparently 'simple' alphabetical order would seem to suggest.

The 'thesaurus' is a reference tool which has been specially devised to help with the selection of indexing terms and, by extension, search terms. The thesaurus lists, alphabetically, indexing terms, but also reveals relationships between terms and thus 'prompts' the searcher by indicating other terms which might be consulted when searching. Here is an illustrative, sample entry for 'Water sports':

WATER SPORTS
    Broader Terms   Sports
    Narrower Terms   Boating
                               Sailing
                               Swimming
                               Waterskiing
                               Windsurfing
    Related Terms   Air Sports

Note the way in which relationships between terms are indicated and compare this with the straightforward alphabetical list of terms shown bove. Although not fully developed, it is obvious that a classified, hierarchical structure is reflected in this thesaurus entry, that is:

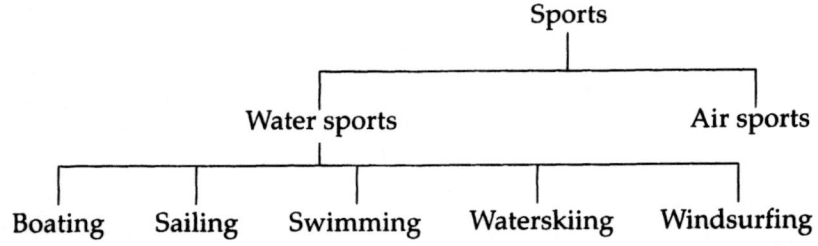

The American *Subject headings used in the dictionary catalogs of the Library of Congress* (LCSH) is also a list of headings which attempts to show relationships and which is devised to help with the selection of subject headings, but this work has been strongly criticized because of the lack of underlying classificatory principles. The most recent edition of LCSH introduces a new format with accepted thesaural abbreviations (such as BT = Broader term, NT = Narrower term, RT = Related term) but the criticism remains: 'The fact of the matter is that the LCSH list is not a thesaurus, not any more ow than it ever was' (Dykstra, 1988). However, the move to try to make LCSH appear more 'thesaural' appears to indicate that the United States now recognizes, albeit only partially, the value of classification for subject retrieval.

A thesaural facility can, in fact, be built into an automated system, so that when a search statement finds no relevant documents, the computer will say to itself: 'Ah, there's nothing under those search words, but what else can I try?' It will then consult the thesaurus and continue the search under appropriate related terms.

Thus, because the best thesauri are based upon classificatory principles, even where the use of alphabetical search terms is concerned, classification has a significant role to play.

Full text databases

Despite the above, Burton, perhaps playing devil's advocate, argues that in the age of the Internet and the World Wide Web it is no longer necessary to teach information professionals classification (Burton, 1997). Today, online systems provide not only citations for works in which information might be found but also contain abstracts or the full text of articles, documents, books, and so on. It is now possible to search a complete text, even a large work such as an entire encyclopaedia, for a single word, that is full text searching. Such databases are available on compact discs (CD-ROMs) as well as online over international networks such as the Internet. Burton maintains that 'Internet search engines can rapidly find the growing volumes of information created and stored electronically using full text retrieval techniques. These search engines ... are capable of handling complex search strategies with Boolean operators' (Burton, 1997).

The use of Boolean operators simply means the linking together of terms by means of operators such as AND and OR. Thus a search for 'Venice AND Climate' would find all items which had been indexed, or which contained, *both* of these terms. A search for 'Venice AND (Climate OR Weather)' would find items which had been indexed under 'Venice' and *either* 'Climate' or 'Weather'.

What Burton apparently fails to recognize is that even Boolean searching involves an element, albeit a minor element, of classification. To take a practical example, let us imagine that a user searches for the keyword 'Computers'. This search might result in too many items being found and, because of this, the system response might be:

COMPUTERS   items matched 956
To narrow the search, enter more terms

The user might then link 'Computers' with 'Education' and enter:

EDUCATION   items matched 378
To narrow the search, enter more words

There are still too many items retrieved, or 'hits', so the user enters:

LIBRARIANSHIP   items matched 23

That's more like it; there is now a manageable number of items to view which could deal with the subject 'Computers in education for librarianship'.

If we examine what has happened here, this type of searching, although Boolean in that the user is searching for 'Computers' AND 'Education' AND 'Librarianship', can be seen also as a type of classification in that the user is, in effect, identifying characteristics of a subject in order to bring like items together and separate unlike – the basic principle of classification.

The above Boolean search could be represented thus, the shaded area representing documents which have been indexed under all three terms:

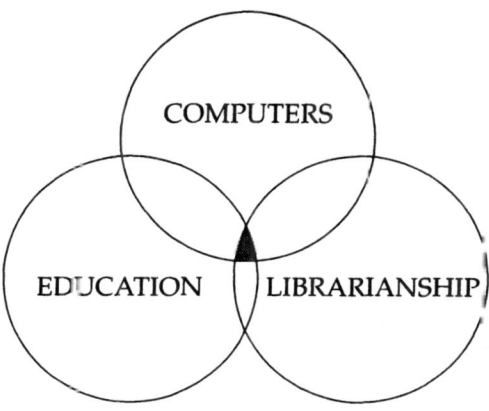

Despite the wide use of Boolean in online searching, not everyone is convinced that it is the best search methodology. Hildreth, for instance, states that

> Much research and experience with Boolean retrieval systems ... indicates clearly and repeatedly that Boolean search formulation syntax and retrieval techniques are not very effective in search performance and not very usable or efficient search methods for end-users ... Determined explorers and the just plain curious need a flexible, rich, contextual subject search and browsing mode which offers plenty of navigation and trail blazing options. (Hildreth, 1989, p. 19)

Schneiderman (1997) maintains that 'until recently, computer scientists argued that the best way to search for information on the Web was by using keyword searching ... But keyword searching often fails miserably'.

There is one word in the first of the above quotes which implies that classification must have a more significant and direct role to play over and above the subtle link with Boolean searching, and that word is 'contextual'. Imagine that a user searches for the term 'Churches' and gets the response:

No items found

Try a more general term

If the user is interested in the church as a physical entity, then, using a similar strategy as in the manual search for 'Roses' already described, he or she might enter the more general, broader term 'Buildings' or perhaps 'Architecture'. Clearly, this type of searching is making use of classification and, where a hierarchical relationship such as this is concerned, the diagrammatic representation would be very different to the Boolean diagram shown above. It would appear thus:

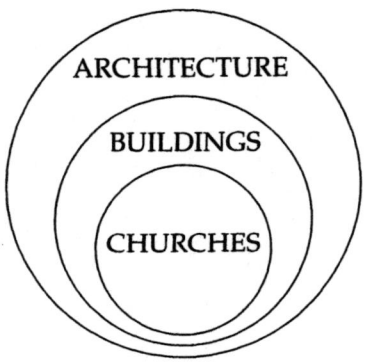

This sort of relationship is therefore not conducive to Boolean-type searches but requires some more explicit form of hierarchical classificatory facility.

The distinction between the two kinds of inter-term relationship described here equates with the syntactical (or *a posteriori*) and thesaural (or *a priori*) relationships described in the international standard ISO 2788–1986. The thesaural, or *a priori*, relationship, this standard states, 'adds a second dimension to an indexing language' and 'the effectiveness of a subject index as a means of identifying and retrieving documents' in any system (including 'those systems in which a computer is used to store and manipulate terms or to identify documents associated with terms') 'depends upon a well-constructed indexing language' (International Organization for Standardization, 1986, p. 1).

The belief that indexing can be done automatically by computer, using the natural language of the title or text, is misguided and it follows that the use of classification is essential for efficient subject access.

Some indexers have already acknowledged the fact that classification can be used for searching the World Wide Web. Dodd refers to the two major trends in accessing resources on the Internet. One involves search engines that exhaustively scan the Web for matches on keywords. The other is the subject-oriented, hierarchical, classification system. 'The explosion of the use of the Internet, particularly via the World Wide Web, has given rise to an interesting phenomenon: the proliferation of semi-professional attempts to give some subject-based access to Internet resources via hierarchical guides (hotlists) such as Yahoo' (Dodd, 1996). 'As a general rule of thumb', Jones (1997) suggests, 'always run your query through both styles of search engine to get the best possible chance of finding what you are after.'

One Web search engine, the hierarchically structured Excite, automatically suggests additional terms to refine your search. If, for example, the initial search is for 'Gold', Excite might suggest other terms such as 'Prospecting', 'Bullion', 'Jewelry' and so on. This is very like the classification-based relative index familiar to librarians, where an indication is given of the various classes where a particular topic can be found, for example:

> Gold : Finance : Economics
> Gold : Jewelry
> Gold : Mining
> ...

Notation

So far, only an implicit mention has been made of the significance of coding or notation, letters, numbers or symbols, which identify particular subjects and place those subjects in an appropriate position in the classification scheme as a whole. All library users will be familiar with this device. Here is an example from the Dewey Decimal Classification, which is hierarchical; the scheme is built up by a process of division, Literature, for instance, being divided by the characteristic of language and then by the characteristic of form:

> 800   Literature
>   810   American literature
>   820   English literature
>   821   English poetry
>   822   English drama
>   823   English fiction
>   830   German literature
>   840   French literature
>   . .

This failure to mention notation specifically was done not by accident but by design because it needs to be appreciated, at an early stage, that one can use classification without even thinking about this problem, although that is not to say that notation or coding is unimportant.

Here is an extract from a textbook which shows an example of a simple, illustrative, classification scheme for soups:

SOUPS

Manufacturer (first digit)
    1 = Heinz
    2 = Batchelors

Type (second digit)
    1 = Tinned
    2 = Condensed
    3 = Powdered

Size (third digit)
    1 = $1^{1}/_{2}$ pints equivalent
    2 = Cup-a-soup

Flavour (fourth digit)
    1 = Tomato
    2 = Chicken
    3 = Minestrone

This is an example of what is known as a 'faceted' classification scheme. Such a scheme breaks down or analyses subjects into constituent elements and then leaves it to the classifier to construct classification numbers for more complex subjects by combination or synthesis. Thus, from the above extract, it can be seen that 'Batchelors powdered tomato cup-a-soup' would be classified as 2321.

This extract is not taken from a librarianship textbook but from Taylor's *Computer Studies* (Taylor, 1991, p. 54), a GCSE school textbook. Taylor is not the only author outside librarianship and information work who goes to the trouble of explaining the nature of classification. Clifton and Sutcliffe, in their *Business Information Systems*, describe hierarchical and faceted classification and include related practical exercises. The authors maintain that 'For practical purposes, it is impossible to identify, uniquely and unerringly, even as few as a thousand different entities if only their descriptions are available' (Clifton and Sutcliffe, 1994, p. 320). 'In a computer-based business system, it is inevitable that code [that is, classification] numbers (which can include alphabetic characters) are needed' (ibid.).

If business and computer experts consider classification so essential, its worth being manifest not only in faceted classification techniques but also in other areas such as hierarchical database management systems and data modelling, then surely it is also vital that librarians and information workers also continue to recognize its merit.

Notation, then, can solve terminological problems and allow complex subjects to be represented by more simple coding. For example, using the Dewey Decimal Classification, a search for 598.2 would find 'Birds',

'Ornithology' and 'Aves'. Also using Dewey, a search for 670.427 would equal a search for 'Computer control of factory operations in manufacturing various products' and, using the British Catalogue of Music Classification, a search for QPG would equal a search for 'Suites for solo piano'.

Some of the special facilities introduced to improve term searching in computerized systems can be adapted for use with classification numbers. An example is the 'truncation' device, which allows searching on word stems, for example a search for 'Comput*' would find 'Computer', 'Computers', 'Computing', 'Computerization' and 'Computerisation'. This same device can also be used on classification numbers as a means of broadening a search. Where the previous example of 'Churches' is concerned, in the Dewey Decimal Classification this topic would be classified at 726.5. Truncation would allow the search to be widened progressively:

Searching for:
- 726.5 would equal a search for 'Churches'
- 726 would equal a search for 'Religious buildings'
- 72 would equal a search for 'Architecture'

Some research has been concerned with the use of the complete classification scheme for online searching. The record of an item could contain the class number, the subject terms which are shown alongside the class number in the classification schedules and the relevant subject index entry from the scheme's index. The user would then be able to conduct a search in various ways: by class number, or by 'keywords' or phrases from the alphabetical subject terms or subject index entry. A facility for browsing forwards or backwards through the index to the system would also assist in the identification of related topics.

Conclusion

This chapter has presented examples of some of the ways in which classification might be used in information management. It has sought to convince the reader that classification is an essential device for the organization and location of materials and retrieval of the information contained therein.

The imminent demise of the book in its separate physical form is not envisaged and therefore the need for classification, as a means of organizing material on the shelves and aiding in its retrieval, will continue. In addition, however, it is certain that increasing use will be made of the full-text storage capability, both offline (via CD-ROM and other such media) and online (via networks), which the computer provides. This offers the opportunity to utilize classification in other ways. The computer can, for instance, 'help to synthesise previously fragmented disciplines by establishing new connections between different fields and subfields' (Quinn, 1994).

Scott and Basu (1997), referring to an article entitled 'Enabling students to search and find' (Herring, 1997), write:

> The key to analysing the information need can be provided by teaching the creation of a subject map. This enables users to create a search aid which describes content and expresses subject relationships and hierarchies. This aid enables them to decide on words which will act as search terms in the whole variety of tools and media. Of course, librarians are already familiar with this process which is at the heart of classification.

Because of the librarian's long experience and expertise in information handling, Schneiderman, who is not a librarian, tells us 'The reality is that librarians have a lot to offer the Information Age. Librarians have been managing complex information for over 200 years. If we were smart, we'd let librarians rule the Net [that is, the Internet].' This is, he contends 'in the long run, the only way the Net will rise to its true potential' (Schneiderman, 1997).

At a meeting of the Classification Research Group (1994), it was stated that 'retrieval rested ultimately on the organisation of knowledge via classification' and 'a librarian ignorant of classification was like a doctor ignorant of biology'. In fact this meeting went even further than merely supporting the continued inclusion of classification in education for librarians:

> We enter the 21st century with the corpus of knowledge growing at a frightening pace. The attendant problems of selecting material from it and deciding just what parts of it might be regarded as an essential core in education is already forcing reappraisals of the national curriculum ... a very strong case could be made for making classification part of such a core.

Many people, therefore, prominent and non-prominent, within librarianship and outside librarianship, regard classification as a major implement. At the start of this new millennium, the question is whether their voices will be heeded. If they are, the research task will be to decide how classification can best be used to help harness, manage and exploit the information explosion.

References

Burton, Paul (1997), 'The decline and fall of "Cat. & Class." ', *Catalogue and Index* (124 Summer), p. 9.

Classification Research Group (1994), Minutes of the 297th meeting held at University College, London, on Friday July 15th (unpublished minutes).

Clifton, H. O. and Sutcliffe, A. G. (1994), *Business Information Systems*, 5th edn, New York and London: Prentice Hall.

Courtenay, Chris (1994), 'Indiana Jones and his homely crusade', *Daily Mail Weekend* (16 July), pp. 4–5.

Dodd, David G. (1996), 'Grass-roots cataloging and classification: food for thought from World Wide Web subject-oriented hierarchical lists', *Library Resources and Technical Services*, **40** (3), 275–86.

Dykstra, Mary (1988), 'LC subject headings disguised as a thesaurus', *Library Journal*, **113** (4), 42–6.

Herring, James (1997), 'Enabling students to search and find', *Library Association Record*, **99** (5), 258–9.

Hildreth, Charles R. (1989), *The Online Catalogue: developments and directions*, London: Library Association.

Huestis, Jeffrey C. (1988), 'Clustering LC classification numbers in an online catalog for improved browsability', *Information Technology and Libraries*, **7** (4), 381–3.

International Organization for Standardization (1986), *Documentation: guidelines for the establishment and development of monolingual thesauri*, 2nd edn, Geneva: International Organization for Standardization (ISO 2788-1986).

Jones, Neil (1997), 'Searching the Web', *PC Home*, (63), 60–64.

Maltby, Arthur (1975), *Sayers' Manual of Classification for Librarians*, 5th edn. London: André Deutsch.

Norman, Barry (1997), 'Why Ford sticks to what he does best', *Radio Times* (12–18 April), p. 46.

Quinn, Brian (1994), 'Recent theoretical approaches in classification and indexing', *Knowledge Organization*, **21** (3), 140–47.

Schneiderman, R. Anders (1997), 'A non-librarian explains why librarians should rule the Net', *Information Outlook*, **1** (4), 34–5.

Scott, N. and Basu, A. (1997), 'Let's get adult about information skills', *Library Association Record*, **99** (8), 428, Letter.

Sellers, Robert (1993), *Harrison Ford: a biography*. London: Hale.

Taylor, Graham (1991), *Computer Studies: GCSE*, 3rd edn, (Macmillan work-out series), London: Macmillan.

2 Organizing knowledge: the need for system and unity

Arthur Maltby and Rita Marcella

The purpose of classifying knowledge, or the items which house it, has always been closely concerned with saving time. In this century, this factor is most significant. For there certainly are still annual increases in that vast output – so variable in quality and relevance – of local, national or global facts and ideas. And, in terms of the technology available, there is a widening range of choices to help identify or present material. Furthermore, new difficulties are presented by a huge body of 'sub-literature' – much of it potentially ephemeral – emerging in purely electronic form. In the light of these factors any absolutely essential commodity which remains in limited and fixed supply becomes infinitely precious. For many seekers of knowledge or information, that key commodity is undoubtedly 'time'.

Time is often scarce

Sometimes phrases are uttered to the effect that people in post-industrial societies, those with increased leisure opportunities in particular, have much more scope for a whole variety of activities. Such assertions are true in a sense, yet it is important to remember that no amount of machine wizardry or other innovation is going to give any individual more than 24 hours in a day. And our modern world, in both its business and leisure aspects, is so rich in alternatives as to how those hours can be spent. That is as true for time spent on 'information retrieving' as anything else. Thus it is that the aforementioned torrent of knowledge (valuable segments sometimes being half-concealed within a composite physical entity), along with enhanced means of access to it, heavily underlines the need to use time effectively.

This leads to major questions. How can the first result of any searches within knowledge's megastore be sieved, assessed and reduced to a manageable package, suited to the needs of the individuals requiring it, so that their time is saved without material loss? Can all relevant associations of linked topics, in the context of a particular enquiry, be achieved? What about controlling the confusion created by the vagaries of natural language?

Any worthwhile answers must give rise to consideration of the principles of order, structure and complex subject relationships – principles which are at the heart of the classifying process. In some cases, these principles may be obscured by the sheer power of modern information networks. For some people it is always the second letter of IT that is writ large, despite the fact that information, or knowledge, is our sought end-product and technology simply the method for reaching it. Certain electronic systems may re-invent some of the traditional principles for subject structuring; others, relying on the sheer scale of technological capacity, may just ignore them.

Fortunately there are some who do address this need positively via increasing technological emphasis on the development of scanning devices, filtering tools or 'intelligent agents'. In considering such controls, the familiar metaphor of future possibilities as an information superhighway is relevant. It will be very heavily populated with traffic. The idea of few signposts and prompts, or no real structure thereon, is unthinkable. One may exit too early, make detours which are expensive in terms of time consumed, be diverted to a destination much less satisfying than that sought . . . or even crash!

Library and information services, most of which are either well served or held in thrall by a system with a strong traditional base, seem very limited in their ability to influence matters. After all, some of their practices as well as the classification schemes used have nineteenth-century roots. And many people think of these services as essentially and permanently book-oriented, thus often misunderstanding or seriously underrating the potential contribution of library practitioners to the dynamic information world of today and tomorrow.

Indeed some modern, technically minded individuals may well look blank if told that principles are needed to focus and control retrieval processes. Perhaps such a statement sounds quaint to them – as though one were insisting upon preliminary cleansing rituals with a vaguely moralistic ethos, or making an arcane plea for old-fashioned 'information-retrieval table manners', long superseded by machines. Yet it must be reiterated that there will always be a need to save enquirers' time.

For there is that danger of over-kill which we see, for example, when chess expert and columnist Nigel Short (1997), surfing the Internet and getting 20 000 entries on offer, complains that 'inclusiveness comes at a cost to comprehension'. Information specialists have no difficulty in finding parallels. Gilchrist (1997), taking up what he agrees is 'an admittedly silly search' to make his point most vividly, tells us that his consultation of the Internet under 'classification' yielded 500 000 hits! Nevertheless, to the information laity, 'people in the street', the impressive capabilities of modern information technology may seem to be the only thing that matters. 'My son, who is a doctor, now accesses all medical literature on his computer... he gets details of simply everything,' says a much-impressed man, while sipping his pint in the local bar. But it sounds so dreadfully daunting; would one want to see it all, even if there were time to do so?

Possibly, of course, in this latter example there was some inbuilt system for effective sifting and selection to match individual user requirements – of the need for which that proud father was entirely unaware, or which was ignored within the shorthand of his casual conversation. Alas, what might seem to be the pearl of greatest price in the retrieval context – dispassionate interpretation of the merit, emphasis and relevance of items – is almost impossible to come by. Yet at least we may have keyword analysis, especially for the content or emphasis of those materials that are composite in their subject coverage. The building up of a set of such key terms and phrases itself necessarily involves classificatory activity.

The need for methodical planning

Knowledge and information are available from computer databases; from broadcasts; from compact discs or cassettes; by word of mouth; from books, journals and other documents. It has always been the purpose of those who 'manage' such a store to access these items effectively. There are various tools for that purpose, of which classification is merely one. These tools have a natural congruence. They ought to be used in effective combination, although often they are not. All too frequently the practice of hard-pressed librarians or other information managers is haphazard: there is little consideration of how the accessing of their own immediate stock in response to an enquiry (doubtless with the aid of the classification system in use) can dovetail with the use of databases, bibliographies, and subject indexes to the content of journals.

To some extent, even the inevitable compartments arising within the professional curriculum – 'reference work' almost always being divided from 'cataloguing and classification' – could have contributed to artificial distinctions. They may have unintentionally obscured what should be seen as the essential unity of all materials and methods for organization and retrieval.

If one were to range the whole twentieth century, seeking out professional writings that have been less influential than they should have been, one choice might be an article by Swank (1944). Perhaps being published in wartime led to its neglect; perhaps some people thought the theme all too obvious. For whatever reason, his plea for more critical discussion over the interrelationship between classification, catalogue, indexes and bibliographies – made in an attempt to promote their efficient use as essentially complementary tools – seems to have had little effect either on subsequent debate or subsequent practice. The message should perhaps be reconsidered within a modern setting.

Of course, bibliographies or other guides of any substance are themselves usually classified in some sense; they may not carry notation, but they seek to subdivide their subject into helpful categories – and to provide annotation, if possible, to justify the placing of any item within a particular category. While subject specialists may sometimes quarrel over exactly what are the best subdivisions for a bibliography within their area, all agree that such a systematic approach is essential to help enquirers move through a mass of material in order to find the items most relevant to them.

Faced with a subject request of some substance, a methodical approach becomes essential. How quickly is the information wanted? Can we supply it from our own resources to hand? Which tools do we use in the light of this particular request and how do they complement each other? Whether or not classification on the shelves or in catalogues plays a prominent part in tackling any one particular request of this kind, the ideas of structure, prompting, and time-saving that lie behind all classification are crucial.

'Technology' should be taken to mean not only hardware and software, but also the system and technique of knowledge management. Classification is about being systematic, as well as about individual 'schemes'. The latter are featured more within the professional training given in some countries and institutions than in others, but 'system' itself is at the heart of most effective information provision. And being systematic means knowing which tools to use in response to a given enquiry and in what combination. The total unified system that is at the information specialist's command may well be unobtrusive – the knowledge seeker is interested in results, not techniques – but it should be there and working well.

Douglas Foskett once (1952) suggested that the word 'classification', within the context of libraries, might well be replaced by 'systematic arrangement'. The argument was good, although the older term was too well established to be ousted. That awareness of many subject relationships and attempt to display the major ones that we call 'classification' should be seen as but one 'systematic' tool among many – all working together in a total system or strategy for effective retrieval. As for classification schemes as such, one is sometimes asked: as many students will not encounter the fully faceted ones when they are practitioners, why do these need to be known?

Part of the answer lies in the fact that they alone take the idea of 'systematic arrangement' to its logical conclusion. In terms of uncompromising adherence to a rigorous application of principles, they are the most committed. Of course, no classification can emphasize all relationships, but had those tangible products of research, the fully faceted systems, arrived on the scene at an earlier date, their use would be much greater. For it is these schemes that have complete predictability, revealing most clearly the subject relationships that have been chosen for regular emphasis and those which have not. In this respect, they point us to the way in which any classification should be used and make that way easier – in them we can note the 'distributed relatives' more readily and then find other means to cope with these.

The fruits of research carried out by individuals and groups have often been only partly assimilated by well-established systems because what is almost a scientific law – their need for stability from edition to edition is directly proportionate to the number of institutional users – means that the full implications are too drastic to be incorporated. The history of classification shows that if a scheme ever dies, it is on the grounds of poor efficiency (by which is meant administration or finance factors) rather than theoretical effectiveness – employing the best principles. Nevertheless, research into new methods and systems has taught us a great deal concerning what classification is (or should be) all about. It may be noted here in passing that technological developments will make efficiency more within the grasp of the schemes, in particular offering the potential for electronic storage of schedules and more regular updates, although it remains to be seen whether such support will be of greater advantage to the publishers of general or special schemes.

Librarians or other information managers with stock on shelves must seek to know just what the classification they do use succeeds in collecting and what it inevitably scatters. Then, conscious of the need for a systematic approach, they can use other means as necessary to atone for the scattering, demonstrating the normally less prominent associations of topics when these are needed, or even highly unconventional linkages via the use of the other tools at their disposal. In many working situations, this sense of a unified approach is missing from the processes in knowledge seeking, so there is no conscious awareness of the potential for the components in information retrieval to be complementary. Pressure of work or ingrained bad habits override the idea of 'total system'. To adjust a Ranganathan phrase slightly – while using it fully in the spirit he intended – reliance sometimes becomes placed too much on chance or upon one individual's retrieval flair rather than on an underlying scientific method.

Thus it is, as professionalism is unwittingly eroded, that classification may be relegated to becoming just a very broad system of physical item display, or even seen as a 'necessary nuisance' which the information manager has inherited; that some of the other tools for retrieval may be underestimated or overlooked; or that the systematic approach itself may be discarded. Bearing in mind the world's knowledge flood, the need to choose and assess carefully from what is in it, and enormous time pressures, this 'system failure' cannot be afforded. Even the most technological future possible cannot evade the need to select and relate material.

Of course, appropriate flair is an asset, as is relevant subject knowledge along with a zest for finding the most appropriate subject resources. But these things should always be an addition to – rather than a substitute for – a methodical approach that uses the various weapons within an information retrieval armoury in effective combination, recognizing that there must be harmonious links between the various strands of technical services. In terms of needing specialist staff on duty, we should not be over-reliant on Lindsay's knowledge of specific themes contained within individual video cassettes in our collection, Mary's occasional inspirational hunches, or Neil's prodigious memory. Things that are worth knowing can be indexed or otherwise noted for the benefit of all the team.

The essential point here is that special flair and knowledge are a bonus to the system; whether these things are present or absent, a 'codified' procedure for system synergy should be there to undergird each subject search. This must be susceptible to change and refinement, incorporating responses to the challenge posed by new information modes or media.

Some problems in classifying

Classifying material costs money. Thus the scheme of classification in use simply must be made to work for its keep. Its ability to do so depends both on its own merits and the willingness of staff to apply it. There must be definable benefits to those who browse at shelves or in classed catalogues; the knowledge possessed by staff of a scheme's structure should be turned to good account in 'making connections' for the retrieval of information. This means more than broadening or narrowing down a search appropriately within a set hierarchy. For the staff of any given collection, it means appreciating, perhaps by the aid of prepared notes based on past experiences, by special indexing, or by technological assistance, the existence of those kinds of unusual relationships which often challenge or evade formal classifying.

To use simple examples, there is a need to recognize, when a booklet on an early blues singer is classed in the music or biography section, that this may also be appropriate for studies of black women's achievements in the twentieth century; that any person about to visit Italy is likely to be interested in language, the arts, and key economic facts as well as geography. And books by such writers as Richard Dawkins, Steve Jones or Paul Davies, rightly placed in the sciences, have considerable implications within the broader view of modern religious studies. One of the present writers was quite recently investigating the work of a most talented, but little-known Scot (J. M. Robertson, 1856–1933). That quest began with literary studies, but soon led on into aspects of comparative religion, rationalist literature, early twentieth-century British history, and several areas within the social subjects.

Some topics are always prone to the crossing of established disciplines. Any investigations relating to psychology may span many fields because the factor of human attitudes and quirks pervades all subject areas. Ethics is a subject with a class of its own in all schemes, but many ethical studies will invade such sections as sports, warfare, politics or medicine. Then there is the case of very occasional items like 'Computing for nurses'; 'Keeping fit: a guide for the handicapped'; or 'Management techniques, with sections of special relevance for school education'. Both rules and experience show the value of classifying by subject, but in instances like this the special-user appeal can at least be flagged in some way. Then, within total retrieval strategy, the special slant is not lost.

We may, on occasion, have to be able to cope with the kind of request which virtually burrows through the whole classification: 'What can you find for me on the influence of Jews and Jewish ideas on western civilization?' System need not be undermined thereby. If we choose to concentrate upon material on site, a variety of reference sources may provide a start; the use of classification with the relative index, the checking of some key names in the author catalogue, plus staff experience of thematic searches, will take matters much further.

One of the authors just mentioned, biologist Richard Dawkins (1991), has some interesting observations to make about all attempts to take classification, as used within his specialism, into the world of books or other knowledge packages. He emphasizes that the problem of organizing these entities is worth tackling, but adds that 'there is no single classification system which, in a world of perfect information, would be universally agreed as the only correct classification'. Very much aware of the many potential links and overlaps which will always exist, he goes on to wonder 'whether librarians . . . are particularly prone to ulcers'.

Any thoughtful response to his wondering might emphasize that this matter indicates why the term 'systematic arrangement' might be preferable, the failure of bibliographical systems to mirror the perfection of classificatory structures within the life sciences being exactly why Jevons, in the nineteenth century, called the classifying of books 'a logical absurdity'. Our response should add that problems are greatly lessened if classification is complemented correctly by other tools within a planned and monitored retrieval system.

Classification: a servant

Naturally the day-to-day process of classifying by one system or another (and noting the outcome) cannot be justified if its whole theoretical basis is simply a quasi-philosophical intellect-stretcher intended to give additional academic rigour to an information science curriculum. This is an appropriate place to mention briefly those personal factors which are often neglected when listing the potential limitations or flaws of classification. For from time to time, the process has been accused – often in colourful language or metaphor – of being a luxury which contributes to the image of an introverted profession; of fostering esoteric rather than meaningful research and reflection; or of existing as a nugatory activity 'behind the scenes' – indulged in by those with 'a passion for order' as an excuse to evade dealing directly with (sometimes difficult) customers.

Such an assertion as this last is reminiscent of an amusing passage by Bertrand Russell in a paper about an American philosopher (reprinted in Olin, 1992), where reality is contrasted with its mere representation. His chosen analogy concerns a vast library and its representative, the catalogue. Someone engrossed in back-room work is imagined as saying that this catalogue, although only a proxy, is the really important thing – the stock has become just useless lumber. Russell wryly adds that such a person has 'naturally lost all taste for reading'.

Caricature is always based on an element of truth, and it is not impossible to find examples of credulous infatuation making people more interested in the means than the end. Incidentally, the very same kind of phenomenon occurs when one discovers an access point to the computerized catalogue in a library monopolized by someone who is far more interested in experimenting with keyboard and program than in reaching information. Nerds of all varieties please note!

It is wrong, of course, to judge any technical aid by its abuse. Nor is there ever any excuse to be neophobic. Such fulminations as this, concerning misapplication, are no more intended to deny or underestimate the value of the computers than they are to deny the value of classification or cataloguing. No wise person would fail to see how much computer technology has accomplished in the field of knowledge retrieval or the potential to achieve much more: machines have added not only speed and capacity, but also valuable new dimensions to information-searching processes. Machine-held files can bring to the fore at will many relationships which would be 'distributed' in any physical display of items. Yet computers, like classification systems and any other technical aid, should always be used appropriately: that fact is writ large within the basic idea of having a total system and strategy. And, from time to time, the success of that strategy and the contribution of individual components should be evaluated.

Returning to Russell, his point is clear and relates equally well to classification which, like cataloguing, is merely a means to an end. There is no merit in saying, with the glee of someone who has at last solved a tricky brain-teaser, that one has, after long deliberation, found the ideal location in a scheme to place an 'awkward' item. At least, not unless some important aspect of the content of that item or its relationship to others is subsequently going to be revealed only via that chosen location or the resulting index entries. Moreover, to use any particular classification well one really needs to know something of many classifications. There are even possibilities for beneficial syncretism. For instance, examination of some of the relationships denoted by the colon in any large collection classed by UDC might help managers of other collections to note potential subject linkages not expressed in the scheme they use, yet likely to be helpful within the pattern of typical enquiries which they receive.

As for the traditional catalogue, it may have been an idol for some, but we would do well to glance at one aspect of its positive side. Fifty years ago in a certain large reference library, where material was not on open access, the catalogue worked very hard as the necessary introduction to the contents of unseen stock. Composite works were analysed, hidden relationships between themes being revealed in subtle – at times almost loving – fashion via additional entries or brief footnotes.

There is a potential modern equivalent. Accepting that users need not be restricted to a single physical collection means acceptance that much possibly useful stock is not immediately to hand. How do we discern which is most useful? Enquirer A may be in a hurry and know just what she wants – 'inclusiveness' in the sense of appropriate items being spotlighted, gained without excess in the form of an undue loss of 'comprehension' or of time. Enquirer B naturally does not want irrelevancies, but may be less sure of his exact needs. His research may give him rather more time to follow up hints and relational pointers. Enquirer C just wants to browse advantageously. Clearly, circumstances vary from case to case: search strategy has to be refined in consultation with the customer.

Sometimes highly significant items may be 'buried' within a larger physical entity. In that context of potential hidden treasure, there is surely a need for cooperative activity or work by various national agencies in analysing composite items for the benefit of all. Such a service could point up profitable relationships that might be missed or detect some 'fugitive' pieces of information, qualitatively most significant, subsumed within larger items. For the quantity of what is available should not deflect us from the search for excellence in terms of offering the most appropriate resources. A very simple example of revealing such items might involve a searcher for information on 'The Universal Decimal Classification' being pointed to the McIlwaine paper available within this volume (Chapter 8). But that is merely the broadening of a search within the main classification hierarchy. More complex examples span subject fields: thus, for instance, the enquirer looking for a balanced estimate of the writer Lillian Hellman might be pointed, on the downside, to the scathing account given in that fiery mix of creeds with criticism constituting Paul Johnson's work 'Intellectuals'.

Adding value

Classifying stock by subject content stands or falls by its contribution to added value within an effective service. By locating all subjects and constantly displaying major relationships it obviously does have the capacity to assist very considerably. But it has a much better chance of contributing fully when its potential is perceived fully by staff, when weaknesses are recognized and covered, and when it is seen as one component in a total system where components are expected to work together. This concerns establishing priorities; having a clear strategy; and anticipating user needs and future subject associations as far as possible.

Several of the arguments made against classification over the years have gained substance from frequently observed failings. Other problems have arisen from antiquated practice. Alas, some collections, if we may adapt a quotation from St Paul, might be seen as 'having a form of classification, but denying its power'. It was not so many years ago that an establishment was found which had only recently desisted from using the last edition of Dewey actually published in his own lifetime. Such was most curious practice, if intended as a personal compliment to a man who stood for dynamism and innovation.

The perception and application of 'classifying' must be linked to grasping its place within a total information-gathering or knowledge-revelation strategy. Provided the processes concerned are not too narrowly defined, the mental or physical associations of themes which denote classification of one sort or another will be seen to be a pervasive and regular activity. Systematic order of stock on shelves is but a useful starting-point. It is of great assistance to the browser, helping considerably to reveal what is in a given collection and is immediately available. Yet, beyond that function, there is much other work which classification can be given and to which it will respond.

The best services will be glancing continually at every way in which their classification might be helpful. They will also, in seeking appropriate resources for learning or leisure, often look well beyond what is on site – searching to access sources which suggest and evaluate what might be most appropriate. They will increasingly seek to produce some of the facts required by an enquirer directly on screen by means of specialist databases or computer networks. They will attempt to group, separate, or relate items in responding to a subject request, while (it is hoped with ever-increasing skill) shaping the end-product to meet user needs. When an approach adopted for an enquiry sets a precedent which could be helpful for the future, they will make suitable brief 'case notes'.

There is also the question of keeping any subject quest flexible yet in manageable proportions: the capacity for irrelevance is almost limitless and some databases seem to offer a pandemonium of noise or distraction in the form of the unwanted. Such control activities as are used to quell these factors are themselves essentially the offspring of a systematic approach or the 'classifying' mind. Of course, there are much more overt uses of classification than this. Where a search is vast and truly international, one or another of the established classifications may itself have a different and prominent role as a 'neutral' switching device in the context of overcoming language barriers.

Conclusion

Future knowledge management situations will be less reliant on items in the immediate store. The content of many suitable resources, or substantial extracts from them, will be available via electronic display and mailing. While this may have important implications for the delving and browsing associated with traditional research methodologies, the need for sorting and 'classing' material to maximize relevance is unaffected – indeed it is heavily endorsed by such developments. This fact may sometimes need to be emphasized to the unwary searcher by the information professional acting as intermediary. Pressures of time and problems of choice will call for classification and other technical services to be used in a more flexible and imaginative way than ever before. It can be predicted with complete confidence that the human factor will always be with us, making imperative the endeavour to build individual flair into 'system' so that it benefits all. It should be seen from this that classification is far more than the application of any scheme or notation: it relates to all our physical or mental attempts to group material or ideas appropriately in order to meet customer needs expeditiously.

Hidden behind all technology, if we use that word largely in the sense of hardware, there remains much scope for good technique; likewise in potential support of all individual systems (classified or otherwise) lies the skill of an individual to make mentally any appropriate subject link and – if need be – to bring that linkage to fruition. These things can be built upon via a fully systematic approach to all storing and finding. The strands of technical services need to be viewed constantly as parts of a whole, in which what each can or cannot do, and how they interact, is noted. Gaps or weaknesses can then be offset. Without distorting whatever is on offer, we must always focus on the relevant and bear in mind the constant pressures upon the enquirer's limited time. Advocacy of classification in all its guises, as being crucial within such planning, is not an excuse for introspection, but a clarion call for that rigorous 'system and strategy' application of which it is itself an integral part.

Glancing well into this century, one can be confident that the 'big three' dynastic-type general systems in use now, however old and creaky they may at times, or in part, appear to some critics, will have faced and surmounted new challenges; they will be available for our successors. However, aside from them and their potential rivals, the ability constantly to make relevant subject associations is fundamental to the work of all information or knowledge 'brokers'. The classificatory principles inherent in exploring and structuring subject relations are at the very heart of every task concerning the sensible sifting of a mass of material. They seek to provide an appropriate and discriminating selection of material along with potential time-saving for the user of the service. Thus even in the highly unlikely event that bibliographical schemes as we know them should one day collapse, the kind of activity called classification would endure.

Furthermore, although document-based services may diminish, user expectations (in terms of time and cost factors) for accessing relevant and useful information are likely to remain paramount. Thus there is now most certainly an extra dimension to consider. The linear, single-place approach of the great traditional library collection can be replicated in the virtual library, where the searcher can negotiate in a physical environment equating with his or her subject needs, despite being in a non-physical or virtual one. Classification may thus find a new form of outlet in the Information Society. It may there accomplish what it never fully could on the shelves of libraries – by helping to translate invisible electronic collections of material into a visible sequence of subjects with a spatial relationship that closely corresponds to each user's needs.

References

Dawkins, Richard (1991), *The Blind Watchmaker*, London: Penguin Books, pp. 257, 260.

Foskett, D. J. (1952), 'Classification and systematic arrangement' (reprinted in his *Science, Humanism and Libraries*, Crosby Lockwood, 1964, pp. 116–22).
Gilchrist, Alan (1997), 'Review of H. Iyer: Classificatory structures', *Journal of Documentation*, **53** (4), September, 431–2.
Olin, Doris (ed.) (1992), *William James' Pragmatism in Focus*, London and New York: Routledge. (Russell's analogy is related on pp. 202–3.)
Short, Nigel (1997), *The Sunday Telegraph*, 6 April.
Swank, R. (1944), 'Subject catalogs, classifications or bibliographies?', *Library Quarterly*, **14** (4), October, 316–32.

3 Can classification yield an evaluative principle for information retrieval?

Julian Warner

> Ay, in the catalogue ye go for men;
> As hounds, and greyhounds, mongrels, spaniels, curs,
> Shoughs, water-rugs, and demi-wolves are clept [called]
> All by the name of dogs: the valu'd file
> Distinguishes the swift, the slow, the subtle,
> The housekeeper, the hunter, every one
> According to the gift which bounteous Nature
> Hath in him clos'd; whereby he does receive
> Particular addition, from the bill
> That writes them all alike...
> (Shakespeare, *Macbeth*, c.1606)

The epigraph indicates the value that has been historically attached to subtlety of distinctions in the language or lexicon of information retrieval systems. In this respect, the passage anticipates the principle formulated in modern discussions of indexing and classification that the value of an index term lies in its discriminatory power. In this principle, and in its historical anticipation, there is a strong, although largely unnoticed, contrast with the assumption of information retrieval research, particularly experimental information retrieval, that the performance of an information retrieval system is to be measured by its capacity to deliver relevant records in response to deliberately articulated queries.

The concern here is not, then, with the uses of classification in information retrieval but with the broader question of whether the central principle embodied in the practice and theory of classification and indexing can yield more satisfying design and evaluative criteria for information retrieval systems than the ideas of measuring relevance and recall abilities characteristically assumed in retrieval research. Two paradigms have been distinguished in information retrieval research – the cognitive and the physical – but they share the assumption of the value of delivering relevant records (Ellis, 1996, p. 19; Belkin and Vickery, 1985, p. 114). For the purposes of the discussion here, they can be considered as a single, if heterogeneous, paradigm, linked if not united by this common assumption.

The contrasting paradigm implicitly embodied in classification and indexing may finally be incommensurable with that of information retrieval research, with disputes also existing which are not logically resolvable within either paradigm. The approach taken in this chapter will be to suggest: that the alternative principle involving discriminatory power has been held, implicitly and explicitly, in a number of largely separate discourses; that the cumulative effect of recognizing this is to indicate more viable and productive criteria for designing, using and evaluating information retrieval systems; and, finally, that the classical tradition of information retrieval research can itself be assimilated to the new model. In this final respect, the development proposed here is an exemplar of scientific development in which discarded paradigms are absorbed into developing ones, as special cases.

The discourses in which an alternative principle for the design and evaluation of information retrieval systems can be discovered and which are to be covered here are: an emerging, although rather isolated and discontinuous, strand of information retrieval research; in the critique of Aristotelian principles and categories for classification by that unconventional philosopher, Giambattista Vico; in accepted discussions of the principles of classification and indexing; and, perhaps most crucially, in ordinary-language discussion of information systems. The chapter will review information retrieval research, thereby taking the liberty of conflating distinguishable aspects for the purposes of a higher-level discussion, and then indicate that an alternative principle for evaluation can be found in the discourses identified. The value of the alternative model developed will be explored. In conclusion, it will be suggested that the alternative principle and criteria developed can have a liberating effect, allowing theory and practice to interact, and that a productive transformation of the field has been indicated.

Alternative paradigms: information retrieval research

Conventional information retrieval research, particularly in the experimental tradition emerging in the 1950s in Britain and North America, has taken as its founding assumption the principle that an ideal information system should deliver all (and possibly only all) the records relevant to a given information need. In order to evaluate information systems in relation to this desired end, or variations on it, various steps were taken: relevance was stabilized and quantified, sometimes being reduced to a binary or dichotomous variable; and measures of precision and recall, which depend on the prior stabilization of relevance, were developed. But more recent research, partly prompted by technological developments, has questioned the validity of aspects of this paradigm, although more frequently with reference to its subsidiary concepts (relevance) and measures (precision and recall) than with regard to its founding assumption.

The adequacy of the concept of relevance as employed in the older information retrieval research must be (and has been) questioned, because experiments there substitute a measurable phenomenon – relevance as constructed under artificial conditions – for an unmeasurable one – relevance under operational conditions – but fail to demonstrate that there is an adequate correlation between the two. Most disturbingly, it has been suggested that operational relevance is fluid, influenced by intention, context, and other documents seen or read, and simply not amenable to stabilization or, further, quantification (Ellis, 1984; 1996).

The classical measures of precision and recall are also rendered increasingly artificial by the high degree of interactivity enabled by recent information technology developments. How, when searching a CD-ROM database, is the final set of records to be isolated except by a process whose very arbitrariness invalidates it as a component of a measure of system performance? High interactivity and unmediated searching also reduce the need for a query to be fully articulated in advance of searching. There has, too, been a realization that a deliberately stated query (which can be distinguished from an information need or assertion of relevance) may be a methodological requirement for controlled experiment, yet not intrinsic to the information-seeking situation (Heine, 1977), and that it was possible to search without verbalizing an information need.

The classic information retrieval paradigm, and the concepts and measures associated with it, could be preserved, but only at the cost of increasing its distance from more realistic information-seeking situations. It may be that not only are the classical concepts and measures both becoming and being recognized as increasingly artificial but that the founding assumption – that a system should deliver all (and only all) the relevant records – should be re-examined. What is required, then, is not a questioning of concepts within the paradigm, but of its founding assumption, turning what has been received as a given starting-point into an object of enquiry.

To some extent, this has begun to occur within the more recent research into information retrieval. The subtlety and complexity of various kinds of information seeking has been recognized (Swanson, 1988). Most specifically, the principle of exploratory capability, the ability to explore and make discriminations between representations of objects, has been suggested as the fundamental design principle for information retrieval systems (Ellis, 1984; 1996).

On a subjective level, this can be supported by introspection: that what I desire from an information retrieval system is not a possibly mysterious transformation of a query into a set of records, but a means of enlarging my capacity for informed choice between the representation of objects in the given universe of discourse. Such an enhanced capacity for informed choice broadly corresponds to exploratory capability. It could also be regarded as analogous to a sense of cognitive control over, or ability to discriminate between, representations of objects.

One example (which may be fictional in a double sense) can be given of the need for enhanced discriminatory power. At one point in time, a researcher might wish to distinguish the private individual, Samuel Langhorne Clemens, from the author, Mark Twain (perhaps out of interest in his copyright disputes or in his brother's, Orion Clemens's, activities as Secretary to Nevada Territory). What would be valuable for this purpose would be a system which did not conflate these two distinguishable aspects of the individual but enabled them to be differentiated. At a later point in time, the same research might be interested in information on Mark Twain and Samuel Clemens considered as a single entity. An information retrieval system should then be able to differentiate and to link together the occurrences of these different names, as required.

In conclusion to this critique of information retrieval research, the assumption that it is desirable to obtain all, and possibly only all, the records relevant to a given query can be rejected in favour of the alternative principle of exploratory capability or enhanced capacity for informed choice. Introspection supported the value of exploratory capability. Its appeal as an alternative to the established information retrieval paradigm could be strengthened if it could be found, even if only implicitly or in analogous forms, in other, independently developed, discourses.

Vico's critique of Aristotelian classification

A strong, and highly significant, analogue to exploratory capability can be found in Vico's critique of Aristotle. Aristotle's philosophy, as well as being a direct and indirect source for subsequent understandings of genus, species, specific difference, synonymy and equivalence, involved, in some of its aspects, a systematic method of enquiry in order to classify an object. An enquirer was required to ask a series of questions: Does the thing exist? What is it? How big is it? What is its quality? and the like. This method of enquiry was subjected to an incisive critique by Vico:

> Aristotle's *Categories* and *Topics* are completely useless if one wants to find something new in them. One turns out to be a Llull or Kircher and becomes like a man who knows the alphabet, but cannot arrange the letters to read the great book of nature. But if these tools were considered the indices and ABCs of inquiries about our problem [of certain knowledge] so that we might have it fully surveyed, nothing would be more fertile for research. (Vico, 1988, pp. 100–1)

The last clause of that critique deserves emphasis: 'nothing would be more fertile for research'. The rigidity of the method is avoided, while some of its techniques are retained, and it is transformed into a systematic and effective means for enhancing knowledge of an object. Analogously, while rejecting the rigid transformation of a query into a set of records assumed as desirable in information retrieval research, similar techniques can be used to explore the domain of discourse covered by the information retrieval system.

A further supporting analogue can be found in the fictional rather than discursive treatment of rigid classifications in Dickens's *Hard Times*. The logical distinctions exemplified in Bitzer's definition of a horse – 'Quadruped. Graminivorous. Forty teeth, namely twenty-four grinders, four eye-teeth, and twelve incisive... Age known by marks in mouth' (Dickens, 1989, p. 6) – which does resemble nineteenth-century taxonomies for the horse, themselves influenced by the Aristotelian method of definition by genus and species, are presented as harsh (Warner, 1994, pp. 106–8). Outside the restricting enclosure of the town, a different metaphor for knowledge is discernible:

> They walked on across the fields and down the shady lanes, sometimes getting over a fragment of a fence so rotten that it dropped at a touch of the foot, sometimes passing near a wreck of bricks and beams overgrown with grass, marking the site of deserted works. They followed paths and tracks, however slight. (Dickens, 1989, p. 353)

The value of an information system could then be the ability it offers discriminatingly to follow 'paths and tracks, however slight'. Classification schemes themselves (and their analogues in thesaural relations among indexing terms) can then be received not as fixed models of stable entities but as valuable exploratory devices.

A principle of indexing and classification

One acknowledged principle of indexing and classification is that the value of a term is its discriminatory power. By discriminatory power is understood the ability to partition and select from the objects represented within the given universe of discourse. Particular terms or methods of classification will vary with the area of discourse and the focus of interest: most obviously, a factor which differentiates one set of objects from another will not serve to discriminate within either set of objects. Discriminatory power is again analogous to exploratory capability, or, more accurately, a critical factor in enabling progressive and controlled exploration.

Ordinary discourse

Ordinary, informal discussion of information systems is simultaneously highly significant here, yet difficult to produce as evidence. Evaluative criteria may be implied rather than explicitly articulated. Yet when a searcher complains that it is difficult to control the number of records retrieved, a principle of discriminatory power is being invoked. More explicitly, one spoken response to an earlier version of this chapter was: 'that's the basis [capacity for informed choice] on which people use systems anyway'.

Summary

Similarities in themes and principles enunciated or implied have been revealed in largely separate discourses, emerging in information retrieval research, made explicit in Vico's critique of Aristotelian methods of investigation, implied in discussions of principles of indexing and classification, and present, in partly unarticulated form, in ordinary discourse. The mode of expression varies, but an enhanced capacity for informed choice, for effective discrimination, or for cognitive control, was discovered to be valued in all the discourses adduced. Independent agreement with an emerging and rather isolated theme in information retrieval research, of exploratory capability, offers supports for replacing the established emphasis on the delivery of relevant records with such a principle for the design and use of information systems. In some respects, possibly through the influence of concepts of classification and of ordinary discourse understandings, working systems may offer exploratory capability and productive interaction. In Vico's terms, practical understanding has been in advance of theoretical articulation.

Evaluative model

Endorsing the principle advocated can have a liberating effect, revealing the intra-theoretic nature of many disputes within the classic tradition of information retrieval research: it offers the possibility of a deeper understanding of relevance; enables a mutually informing relation between practice and theory; restores man as artificer as a designer and user of information systems rather than cipher of information retrieval research; and can enable the development of more satisfying evaluative criteria.

Disputes over the validity of 'measures' demanded for retrieval system evaluation in the classic tradition of information retrieval research, for instance whether deliberately contrived relevance judgements are adequately correlative with real-world judgements, can now be regarded as intra-theoretic, connected with the theoretical framework imposed, not inherent in the process of information retrieval and not necessarily contributing to an understanding of those processes. In some respects, the construction imposed by the research paradigm may even have inhibited development of understanding of its chosen domain of study. For instance, the methodological need to reduce relevance to assessments, possibly open to quantification, and stable over time, may have inhibited exploration of its many possible dimensions. Some dissenting discussions have insisted on its complex and multifaceted nature (Wilson, 1973; Watson et al., 1973).

A mutually informing and productive relation between theory and practice can be developed. For instance, the practical experience of those indexing procedures or retrieval algorithms which enhance exploratory capability in specified circumstances can inform theoretical development and system design and modification. The divorce of information retrieval research from practice has been noted and sometimes regretted, although less often explained. Now the practical understanding embodied in working systems can be recognized and theoretically developed.

The further question then arises as to whether accepting the principle of exploratory capability has practical implications in terms of the indexing procedures or algorithms for searching to be adopted. An immediate response would be that it does not necessarily have unambiguous practical implications: that the particular indexing procedures and algorithms to be used will be critically dependent on the purpose and context of retrieval, including the cost of indexing and retrieval Crucially for continuity of systems development, techniques identical with or analogous to those currently developed may be used to different ends. It should also be noted that the Boolean logic used in many retrieval systems does, under certain conditions, have the advantage of relative transparency to the searcher. The objection that it is an ineffective way of transforming an information need into a set of relevant records is no longer tenable. It could still be objected that in some applications, for instance with heterogeneous textual material without humanly assigned terms, it gives inadequate control over the representations within the universe of discourse.

A deeper effect is to restore man as an artificer and to recognize the subtlety of the processes involved in information retrieval. Rather than being subjected to a retrieval process beyond immediate control, the searcher is presented with an enhanced capacity for choice and for making recalled sets. The new, and historically unprecedented, potential for enhanced forms of knowing of existing textual material can then be productively explored. For instance, the unrivalled opportunity offered by a full-text database for exploring the semantic mutability of written word forms within different contexts can be pursued.

More detailed evaluative criteria could be developed from the central evaluative principle of enhanced choice, partly by drawing on the understandings developed in discussions of classification. Yet it should be recognized that quantitative comparative measures are unlikely to result. Once the diversity of contexts for information retrieval is recognized, the idea of a single, generally applicable approach to system design, or a single comparative measure of system performance, becomes severely questionable. The best outcome that can reasonably be expected from research and from reflection on practice is a better understanding of the process of information retrieval, which can then be used either to design better information systems or to make more effective use of existing systems.

Conclusion

Replacing the emphasis on the delivery of relevant records with a stress on exploratory capability or cognitive control as a design-and-use principle for information retrieval has a liberating effect. It yields more satisfying evaluative criteria while preserving a strong continuity with previous work, particularly in recognizing the utility of developed information retrieval techniques. Theory and practice, rather than being separate or even antagonistic, are enabled to inform each other. The discourses – of philosophy, classification and ordinary discussion – from which the new principle has been drawn can be brought further to bear upon information retrieval, transforming it into a human science and recognizing its subtlety and significance. A minor, although significant, relief is liberation from the obligation to read works in the classic information retrieval paradigm, except for their emerging signs of self-questioning.

The transformation advocated in this chapter resembles, in some respects, a mathematical revolution and can also be seen as an example of scientific progress. Classically, fundamental transformations of mathematics have preserved the form while modifying the interpretation (Ramsey, 1926); analogously, information retrieval techniques have been preserved but adapted to a new end. More broadly, it has been suggested that discipline exhibits the history of a true science if its earlier stages can be seen as special cases, from the perspective of its subsequent development (Roberts, 1982): in this context, the automatic transformation of a query into a set of records can be seen as a possible support for informed choice, valuable in certain sets of circumstances. Rather than, as Swanson (1988) indicated, 'Waiting for Godot [while failing] to grasp what is now within reach', we can begin to explore the potential for improving human interaction with recorded knowledge.

References

Belkin. N. J. and Vickery, A. (1985), *Interaction in Information Systems: a review of research from document retrieval to knowledge-based systems* (Library and Information Research Report 35), London: British Library.

Dickens, C. (1989 edn), *Hard Times*, edited with an introduction and notes by Paul Schlicke, Oxford and New York: Oxford University Press.

Ellis, D. (1984), 'Theory and explanation in information retrieval research', *Journal of Information Science*, **8**, 25–38.

────── (1996), *Progress and Problems in Information Retrieval*, London: Library Association.

Heine, M. H. (1977), 'The "question" as a fundamental variable in information science', in O. Harbo and L. Kajberg (eds) (1980), *Theory and Application of Information Research* (Proceedings of the Second International Research Forum on Information Science, 3–6 August 1977, Royal School of Librarianship, Copenhagen), London: Mansell, pp. 137–45.

Ramsey, F. P. (1926), 'The foundation of mathematics', in: D. H. Mellor (ed.) (1990). *Philosophical Papers*, Cambridge: Cambridge University Press, pp. 164–224.

Roberts, N. (1982), 'A search for information man', *Social Science Information Studies*. **2**, 93–104.

Swanson, D. R. (1988), 'Historical note: information retrieval and the future of an illusion', *Journal of the American Society for Information Science*, **39** (2), 92–8.

Vico, G. (1988 edn), *On the Most Ancient Wisdom of the Italians: unearthed from the origins of the Latin language: including the disputation with the Giornale de' letterati d'Italia*, Ithaca and London: Cornell University Press.

Warner, J. (1994), *From Writing to Computers*, London and New York: Routledge.

Watson, L. E. et al. (1973), 'Sociology and information science', *Journal of Librarianship*, **5**, 270–83.

Wilson, P. (1973), 'Situational relevance', *Information Storage and Retrieval*, **9** (8), 457–71.

4 Information technology and new directions
Robert Newton

The aim of this chapter is to examine a variety of advances in both the theory and practice of classification with particular reference to the impact of new technology on the development and application of library classification. It will examine these in terms of:

- developments in 'traditional' published schedules
- pragmatic attempts to apply classification to organize digital resources
- developments in the theory of knowledge organization and the impact of this on the direction of research dealing with establishing automatic control over classification and retrieval of large collections of digital documents.

In its widest sense classification deals with the ordering of knowledge and thus can be seen to encompass a range of disciplines, involving the application of tools and theories developed in areas such as philosophy, communication science, lexicography, linguistics, artificial intelligence, computing and mathematical sciences as well as, of course, library and information science.

To a certain extent we have seen a tendency towards the convergence of many themes which were previously seen as discrete concerns of particular cognate disciplines. This has been coupled by a much more proactive approach by the library and information profession to exploring new roles for classification in an online environment in order to demonstrate the continued relevance of professional skills in environments in which information is stored and accessed in electronic form.

Developments in library classification schemes

The development of library classification schemes for shelf ordering for bibliographic classification is not an area in which we should expect any radical changes. The main bibliographic classification schemes – the Dewey Decimal Classification Scheme, the Library of Congress Classification Scheme and the Universal Decimal Classification Scheme (and to a lesser extent the Bliss Bibliographic Classification Scheme and the Colon Classification Scheme) – are now established tools for ordering physical documents for general library collections. In addition, special schemes such as the National Library of Medicine Classification, the Moys Classification scheme (Law), the CI SfB (Architecture and Building) and the London Classification of Business Studies scheme are also firmly established tools for practical classification of documents within specific subject disciplines.

This observation is in no way meant to detract from the solid body of practical work which has been undertaken in the revision and updating of these schemes over the past few decades and which is currently being vigorously pursued by their various editorial committees. In particular, note should be made of the advances in the use of technology to assist in the procedures for updating and distributing these schemes – notably the development of CD-ROM-based systems. Chronologically the first significant development was the Electronic Dewey (Electronic Dewey, 1993), which Trotter contended 'takes us well on the way to the electronic age of classification' (Trotter, 1995). This was fairly quickly followed by the introduction of a Windows version of the product – Dewey for Windows (Dewey for Windows, 1996; updated 1998). Parallel to these developments was the introduction of electronic versions of the Library of Congress Classification scheme – notably the promotion of the Cataloger's Desktop (LC Cataloger's Desktop, 1994) and the introduction of Library of Congress Classification Plus (LC Classification Plus, 1996) and Super LCCS (Super LCCS, 1996).

Obviously using such systems provides advantages in terms of saving shelf space and making the process of classification somewhat easier through the use of novel search interfaces and the application of keyword searching to assist the classifier to use the schedules more easily. However, they cannot really be regarded as examples of a radical intrusion of technology into library practice. Will's discussion of Dewey for Windows, for example, asserts as positive feature the fact that 'the software replicates the procedures that a classifier would adopt when using the bound volumes' (Will, 1997). Surely, however, we should be setting our sights higher and looking for considerably more 'added value' from such software. Certainly it is not possible to agree with Koh's assessment of the impact of such changes when she writes that 'the virtual library promoted by librarians' integrated tools at their workstations is a harbinger of what may develop in the organizational structure of libraries. Its ultimate impact will be a redefinition of libraries, librarians and education for librarianship' (Koh, 1995).

The essential character and philosophy of the schemes for providing a classification of knowledge is to a large extent fixed, but that is not to say that the background to the development of these schemes is not worthy of consideration. The intellectual contribution that has been made over the past century, which has resulted in the successive refinement of bibliographic schemes, should not go unmentioned. Indeed this is an area in which there is still considerable potential as much of the 'new' research and developments in classification have their roots very firmly embedded in the work of such theorists as Cutter, Coates, Kaiser, Metcalfe, Farradane and Ranganathan. The challenge, however, is to take this body of knowledge and apply it to the current environment in which information is being stored and accessed.

Classification of electronic resources

The extension of the use of bibliographic classification schemes to encompass control of access to electronic documents is an area in which there is considerably more development.

The obvious question with which to preface a section such as this is to ask why we require a formal methodology to classify Web resources when there are numerous search engines[1] which already (with varying levels of complexity) permit subject searching of Web documents. The answer to this is obvious, however, to anyone who has attempted to use such search engines to conduct a comprehensive search for information on the Web. The deficiency of search engines is noted by a number of authors. Johns, for example, describes a project at UCSB (University of California at Santa Barbara) which has as its objective the provision of access to Internet resources to supplement the local online catalogue. Commenting on the effectiveness of search engines to retrieve important texts which are available only in electronic format, she says of one case that 'I tried searching this on Yahoo,[2] Excite, AltaVista and InfoSeek and only one of these search engines listed the official Occupational Outlook Handbook as the first source' (Johns, 1997).

Thus whilst we can agree with Lesk's contention that there is scope for libraries to 'augment their collection policies with an understanding of the problems of digital materials' (Lesk, 1997), it appears that currently search engines are not efficient enough tools to provide adequate 'bibliographic control' over such an extended resource base.

At this point it should be noted that to organize Internet resources efficiently it is necessary to be selective and the suggestion that libraries must engage in the Herculean task of comprehensively providing access to all Internet documents or even to be exhaustive in coverage of the whole of a particular subject area is not a practical one. A comparison with the manner in which physical stock is acquired and maintained by libraries shows the basic fallacy of this approach. The idea that all 'documents' which are added to stock should be exhaustively indexed and made available via the catalogue has never been a feasible option, and a huge amount of peripheral or 'grey literature' is not subject to rigorous bibliographic control. The effective filtering of information and an evaluation of its worth is becoming recognized as an important role for the professional librarian. Another 'myth' that has coloured the attitudes of some librarians embarking on Internet classification is associated with the perceived instability of Web documents and value of such resources. This is explored by Jul (Jul, 1997) who argues against the viewpoint that the resources on the Internet are of dubious quality and permanence. Certainly anyone using the Internet is familiar with encountering the 'Error 404, Object not found' message. But this should not detract from the large corpus of solid information which can be accessed from well-established and maintained Web sites. Current developments in Web document management technologies to update links automatically and 'push technologies' to alert users to changes and additions to Web-based directories provide librarians with powerful tools to assist in organization of electronic resources and offer the potential to make available effective electronic SDI services.

A pragmatic approach to selectively organizing and classifying Internet resources is evident in a number of current initiatives and projects (not all based in libraries). The following section examines the issues which are important in the question of whether systematic arrangement by means of a classification scheme offers a solution to the problem of information organization on the Internet rather than attempting to provide a comprehensive overview of all such developments. There is a range of resources which gives more comprehensive coverage of this area and in particular this is done by the Web Directory Guide (http://www.directory.guide.com/) and a discussion of a number of such sites is provided in McKiernan's paper 'Beyond bookmarks: schemes for organizing the web' (available at: http://www.public.iastate.edu/~CYBERSTACKS/CTW.htm). The Telematics Research project DESIRE (DESIRE, 1998) gives a review of the use of classification schemes in Internet resource description. Finally, an extremely useful survey is also provided by van der Walt (van der Walt, 1998), who has conducted an extensive investigation and gives a categorization of Internet guides and directories.[3] Of 45 selected for further investigation he identified 23 using traditional classification schemes (15 using Dewey, 5 using Library of Congress, 2 using the UDC and 1 using the Nederlanse Basisclassificatie) and 22 using broad verbal classes.

It is not proposed that the last category should be dealt with in any detail here. It includes directories such as Yahoo, Excite: Channels, The Argus Clearinghouse, the Britannica Internet Guide and the Magellan Internet Guide. It also encompasses many of the subject gateways which have been developed in the United Kingdom within the Access to Resources strand of the Elib programme: EEVL, ADAM, biz/ed, OMNI, SOSIG, RUDI, CAIN, and IHR-Info. Two other Elib projects ROADS (ROADS, 1998) (Resource Organisation and Discovery in Subject-based services) and CATRIONA (Cataloguing and Retrieval of Information over Networks) (CATRIONA, 1998) are of more significance in the context of this chapter as they focus on the general problem of providing subject access and descriptive information for electronic resources.

The Dewey Decimal Classification has been employed in a number of projects. Examples include the Canadian Information by Subject project, and The Internet Public Library and the Morton Grove Online Webrary. An interesting development is CyberDEWEY, a Web site developed by David Mundie who, although a non-librarian, found that the DDC provided a logical mechanism and a solution to a personal need to organize his own data (Mundie, 1998). This in itself, whilst interesting, cannot really be taken as indicative of the potential of traditional classification schemes to have an impact on organizing the Web.

Several commentators see the UDC as a particularly useful starting-point for organizing Web resources. This is based on the international emphasis that is a feature of the scheme and the fact that the machine-readable format of the scheme is widely accessible to Internet developers (McIlwaine, 1995). The UDC is the basis for the Nordic WAIS/World Wide Web project – a Scandinavian venture which is designed to make use of the machine-readable UDC and, in tandem with developing a common interface to databases which can be accessed on the WEB, uses the UDC vocabulary and notation to index the databases (Ardo et al., 1998). The Directory of Networked Resources (NISS) is very much a 'library-oriented' project and attempts to achieve a professional level of subject coverage by a collaborative system which is channelled through individual libraries in the UK. A resource description template has been devised and this can be completed online. The NISS gateway resources are indexed using the UDC and can be accessed via subject or keyword searches. The UDC and the NISS template are also being employed in indexing the Social Sciences Information Gateway (SOSIG), one of the subject gateways developed within the UK electronic libraries programme. In keeping with the UDC's aim of providing a very detailed synthetic approach to the classification of knowledge, the examples of sites which adopt this classification display a much more rigorous approach to defining the subject of documents, and the close classification evident here contrasts with the fairly simplified notation and lack of detail which typifies the DDC and LC sites.

There are also several examples of the use of the Library of Congress Classification Scheme. The Internet Scout project is based at the University of Wisconsin in Maryland. The Scout Report Signpost (Signpost, 1998) project provides three primary methods for organizing and accessing Internet sites which have been identified as valuable resources for libraries by the Internet Scout project. These provide facilities to:

- search through 'Quick' (full text search of all Scout report summaries) and 'Advanced' interfaces (searching by a variety of fields: author, title, publisher etc.)
- browse using Library of Congress Subject Headings and
- browse using Library of Congress Classification.

Another significant site which is based on the Library of Congress Classification is CyberStacks (CyberStacks, 1998), developed in 1994 by Gerry McKiernan. Several contributors to this volume understandably refer to his work. His endorsement of the LC Classification Scheme (McKiernan, 1997) is mentioned in the chapter on that system (Chapter 9). My own view is that this involves more faith than judgement; that his contention is not validated in either this or his other writings (McKiernan, 1995). And this, to be fair, is a comment which could be equally well applied to a number of other projects that aim to apply standard classification schemes to organize WWW resources.

Problems in classifying electronic resources

In summary, there is a great deal of very useful work being done in this area and there is no doubt that a number of these projects are showing clear benefits to end users in making some sense of the tangled information environment of the Internet.

However, there are two fundamental issues which should be considered:

- the basis for using traditional published classification schedules as a tool to organize electronic collections
- the basis on which such initiatives can be adequately supported in terms of an infrastructure and strategy for their continued maintenance and development.

Traditional schemes in the age of digital libraries

No one would question the need for organization and these projects are all examples of proactive interventions which seek to provide this, but what exactly is the role of the 'traditional classification scheme' in these projects? It is often stated as a truism that the skills of librarians and information workers are important and the unstated assumption is generally that these skills are directly transferable between physical and electronic environments. Unfortunately, all too often when we examine the use of classification in modern technological contexts we find that this assumption is not supported. Generally the guides which use classification, which have been described above, do so in a very limited way. The classification system is used to support arrangement of entries on Web pages to make provision for browsing and in some cases to provide access points for specific searching. However, they are rarely used to provide much more than a broad system of ordering, and often the classification scheme is adopted in a very truncated form. The user often has to progress through numerous screens to follow a hierarchical search for information. Classification should offer much more than this. There would seem to be tremendous scope for developing traditional classification and building on the enormous effort which has been expended in creating manually produced thesauri in order to provide a syndetic structure which could be used as the basis for systematizing hypertext linkage between electronic documents. Vizine-Goetz provides a useful summation of the methods by which online classification data can be used to enhance retrieval (Vizine-Goetz, 1996). These include development of end-user interfaces that employ adaptive methods for displaying classification hierarchies, automatic translation of DDC and LC schedule captions to make them understandable to end users, and the use of links to subject thesauri which are an integral part of classification schemes. This is very much the basis for the argument which is being put forward by Mitchell, who writes: 'It is time to promote our carefully developed, maintained and continuously updated library classification systems as general knowledge organisation tools' (Mitchell, 1998). Woodward notes some dissension from this viewpoint (Woodward, 1996) but, as she observes, the comments made by writers such as Steinberg and Srinivasan are essentially flawed and demonstrate a misconception of how modern classification schemes are maintained and updated. However, there are more serious issues which need to be considered. The main question which needs to be posed when considering how appropriate traditional published schedules are, is whether or not classification systems which were designed to fulfil a specific function with respect to ordering physical collections of documents are appropriate vehicles for ordering and assisting efficient retrieval of materials from a 'virtual library'.

To a certain extent this has already been fairly comprehensively discussed and researched in the literature which examines the problem and mechanisms involved in using classification schemes to enhance subject searching in online public access catalogues. The argument for enhancing access using classification in this case, as advocated by writers such as Svenonius (Svenonius, 1983), Cochrane (Cochrane, 1985), Bates (Bates, 1977) and others, is a very convincing one. However, the outcome of practical projects which seek to demonstrate how this can be done, in particular the results of the DDC Online Project (Markey and Demeyer, 1986), failed to demonstrate the manner in which benefits could be achieved in practice. A full discussion of the use of classification to enhance searching of the OPAC is provided by Marcella (Marcella, 1994) and need not be reiterated here. The assessment by Kowalk of work in this area is very negative but accurately reflects the main problem. He implies that there is a requirement for a radical rethinking of how classification should be developed for online resources and asserts that 'a classification not specifically conceived for an automated library system, and even a classification that is automated from the very beginning, has methodologically immanent and application-related peculiarities that are inconvenient in an OPAC' (Kowalk, 1993).

Essentially the result of research to date should lead us to question the extent to which the application of classification in an online environment requires a reconsideration of the basis on which a scheme for knowledge organization should be designed. Traditional schemes for knowledge representation are essentially linear in their approach. What is required is the development of a theoretical approach to knowledge organization which accommodates the fact that in a digital environment we can provide organization which does not necessarily have to be limited in terms of achieving permanent classifications which seek to 'fix' subjects in terms of allocating them to static sections of a preordained hierarchy or map of knowledge. The inherent flexibility of electronic manipulation of documents or their surrogates should allow a more organic approach to allocation of new subjects and appropriate linkage between subject hierarchies. Hypertextual links can replace conventional references and the cross-classification of documents can be seen as a positive benefit in providing alternative approaches to retrieval rather than an evil which should be avoided at all costs.[4] It could provide a mechanism for reallocating entire areas of 'classification schedules' if required (a concept which would of course be total anathema to librarians who base the organization of physical document collections on established divisions of published bibliographic classification schemes). It should be emphasized that what is advocated here is not a radical departure from traditional library classification schemes and the introduction of a completely new schedule of classification for electronic resources. What is required, rather, is a synthesis of the best features of the major bibliographic schemes, and a much more rigorous approach to consistently implementing faceted principles which promise to provide the flexibility to achieve automatic hypertextual linking of related concepts (Liu, 1990). Returning to what was said earlier in the chapter about the value of the contribution to classification theory over the past century, it is worth noting that the full extent of Ranganathan's distinctive and radical thinking in his numerous books and papers and the significance of the paradigm shift in classification theory which he inaugurated has not yet been fully mined.

Resource-effective classification

The second problem which, it was noted, arises from attempts to apply classification to electronic documents is that, if such classification is to be successful, procedures have to be adopted which, as far as possible, make these developments efficient in terms of resource management.

Commenting in the context of developments in classification within OPACs, Hill noted that such systems must demonstrate both functionality and cost-effectiveness (Hill, 1990). The challenge in an online networked environment is probably greater and it is vitally important that, if we are to extend classification to provide an organizational structure for the Internet, we need to consider this carefully in terms of strategic management of staff and resources. There are a number of reviews of pragmatic approaches taken by individual library services. Articles by Yip and Neuminster, for example, give a useful insight into some of the management issues involved in integrating the control of digital resources into library routines, and discuss identification procedures and selection criteria for 'acquiring' Internet resources (Neuminster, 1997).

Overall we need to balance the reality of everyday working with the need to move forward strategically. How this can be accomplished is not evident in the claims made for classification of electronic resources, and integration of the work involved in developing resources with the traditional work routine in the technical services or cataloguing departments of libraries is rarely mentioned. The problems associated with maintenance of these classified collections and the evaluation of their effectiveness is also an area which is not given adequate discussion in the literature.

In particular, it is important to critically appraise systems which can help to minimize the very staff-intensive input which must be made to create useful tools and procedures to deal with the problem of cataloguing and classifying Internet resources. Woodward quotes the statement of philosophy of The Argus Clearing House (Woodward, 1996) which asserts that 'The Argus Clearing House was founded on the belief that in order to make the Internet a more useful information environment, human effort must be combined with searching and browsing technologies.' However, as Miksa and Doty (1994) remind us, this approach must be balanced against the prohibitively expensive labour costs associated with indexing large collections. It would thus be very foolish to ignore the advances being made in automatic retrieval techniques, natural language processing and artificial intelligence technologies.

Automatic classification of electronic resources

The final area to be considered is the extent to which advances in using automatic techniques for organization and retrieval of electronic documents, or document surrogates, have developed and have had an impact on classification theory and practice. In a recent textbook on classification the authors conclude a chapter which reviews automatic classification techniques by quoting Wellisch's assessment of how far this has had an impact on practice.

> All these quasi-operational 'automatic' projects share a characteristic that might be compared with reports on the manufacture of mechanical birds: after a quarter of a century of trial and error, some models begin to look bird-like, a few can imitate chirping noises, some can flap their wings, but so far none can really fly or sing – a fact carefully hidden behind some dense verbiage, generally in the last but one paragraph of such reports. (Wellisch, 1981)

The situation is currently unaltered in that there are no practical examples which demonstrate how library classification schemes have been overtaken by purely automatic approaches to assigning documents to appropriate subject categories. However, the stakes in developing such systems are now considerably higher and are attracting a great deal of attention. Again, the reason for this is largely associated with the need to provide a practical solution to organizing access to Internet-based resources. A number of authors note the problems raised by the fact that the Internet search services depend to a large extent on simple approaches to indexing which rely primarily on Boolean manipulation of natural-language terms drawn from online documents (Lowry, 1995; McFadden, 1993). Some engines employ weighted relevance measures but there is a general consensus that such techniques are not providing adequate results in terms of precision and relevance.

Thus, whilst this is still an area in which a great deal of experimental research has yet to impact significantly upon users, there is certainly ample evidence that this field of research and development is now becoming regarded as of central importance to 'mainstream' research in classification. Furthermore, developments in this field are being stimulated and supported by multinational corporations such as Digital Equipment Corporation (in developments associated with the improvement of AltaVista) and Sun Microsystems (in an extensive research programme on creating an automatic conceptual indexer) (Fallows, 1996). In the past, methods of automatic classification which relied on clustering methodologies and statistical manipulation were very much hampered by problems because of lack of computing power and limited storage. Estimation of probabilities in most IR systems, which are not experimental, is still incomplete, but there is a growing number of research projects which are attempting to employ derived indexing to support knowledge structuring. These include projects which examine different clustering methods based on:

- statistical co-occurence of terms, some of which propose using traditional classification vocabularies as a means of clustering documents, for example HyPursuit (HyPursuit, 1988) and Scorpion (Shafer, 1996)
- text classification
- linguistic methods using semantic analysis and concept maps
- 'learning systems', such as KBS-CROSS, which use neural network methods to assist browsing and searching (KBS Media Lab, 1988).

The Scorpion research project, based at OCLC, one of the best examples of the development of tools for automatic subject recognition based on established classification schemes, is discussed more fully in the next chapter. It can be seen as similar in concept to the partial match retrieval techniques employed by Larson, who attempted to assign the appropriate LC classification to 'new' MARC records by using a comparison based on the titles and subject headings used in MARC records which had previously been assigned appropriate classmarks. The project also builds on other work which has been done on statistically based document representation and associated algorithms to score and rank retrieval. The role of class integrity or unambiguous subject definition of classes in the success of such a project has already been identified as of critical importance. The results of this research, therefore, should provide a valuable contribution to our knowledge and understanding of the problems inherent in traditional schemes. This in turn should provide a solid basis for the re-engineering of schemes to deal effectively with retrieval in an electronic environment.

A final reason for optimism in this area is the fact that the emphasis of much of the research has become much more 'user-centric'. Ellis provides a very good overview of progress in the information retrieval techniques and gives an insight into the extent of the changes which have taken place in the methodology for designing and evaluating IR systems (Ellis, 1996). Since the early Cranfield tests we have seen the progressive trend towards a more cognitive approach to information retrieval research. The development and experimentation with systems for transaction logging allow us to use technology to good effect in monitoring the manner in which users approach a search for information. The challenge will be to interpret the output from this and make sense of it in terms of developing a model which will accurately accommodate and assist a variety of 'searching styles' to be used as the basis for creating efficient systems for organizing information.

Conclusion

Librarians must strive to become involved in the task of classification of digital materials. Universal bibliographic control is a hopeless ambition within the ever-changing and ever-expanding electronic environment. However, as is evident from various initiatives described above, information professionals can make strategic interventions into the tangled information environment of the Internet. The contribution which they can make needs to be seen not only in terms of how they can develop practical initiatives to classify Web documents using their traditional skills in subject analysis and description, but also in the role which they can have in informing the development of new techniques that rely on automatic approaches to classification.

In a previous age classificationists (makers of systems) had to be 'polymaths' who could assimilate and interpret a range of disciplines to provide structures to deal with the whole of knowledge. As we enter the millennium, the challenge for those involved in classification research is similar in that it is becoming increasingly important that a whole range of research and development work in a variety of disciplines needs to be effectively synthesized. The most important requirement for the information worker in this field will be the ability to comprehend and blend together these strands and, with a sound understanding of both the theory and practice of classification, to design systems which provide solutions to practical problems of arrangement of subjects and documents to facilitate easy retrieval.

Notes

1 A useful guide to a large number of such engines and the key features of how they are used is provided by Falk, *Electronic Library* vol. 15, no. 1, February 1997, pp. 49–55. As with all writings on the Internet, we must interject the caveat that developments in this field are taking place at such a rapid pace that any printed source must be supplemented by electronic sources. A good online source is

provided by Liu – Understanding WWW search tools – http://www.indiana.edu/~librcsd/search/
2 It is interesting to note that this is an example of a confusion which often arises over the distinction between search engines and Web directories (Yahoo being an example of the latter). Yahoo is in fact a collection of Web sites which have been manually reviewed and categorized within subject hierarchies. It would be interesting to note how this approach had fared in comparison with the results experienced via the search engines used, but unfortunately Ms Johns does not expand on which of the instruments used provided the best performance.
3 Unfortunately the review is in Afrikaans and is not translated. However, the article is worth examining because of the large number of useful URLs it provides.
4 This can be seen as contrasting starkly with the policy adopted by the Yahoo project team which allocates only one position for each URL indexed in the directory.

Bibliography and references

Anderson, C. and Hauptman, R. (1993), *Technology and Information Services: challenges for the 1990s*, Norwood, NJ: Ablex.

Ardo, A. et al. (1998), *Improving resource discovery and retrieval on the Internet: the Nordic WAIS/World Wide Web project*. Available at http://www.ub2.lu.se/W4/summary.html

Balas, J. (1996), 'Dewey and the Net', *Computers in Libraries*, **16** (1), 46–7.

Bates, M. (1977), 'Factors affecting subject catalogue search success', *Journal of the American Society for Information Science*, **28** (3), 161–9.

CATRIONA (1998). (Cataloguing and Retrieval of Information over Networks Applications.) Available at http://wp269.lib.strath.ac.uk:5050/cat2/catcontents/index.htm

Chan, L. M. (1995), 'Classification: Present and future', *Cataloguing and Classification Quarterly*, **121** (2), 5–17.

Cochrane, P. A. (1985), 'Preparing for the use of classification in online computer cataloging systems and in online catalogs', *Information Technology and Libraries*, **4**, 91–111.

Cochrane, P. A. (1995), 'New roles for classification in libraries and information networks', *Cataloging and Classification Quarterly*, **21** (2), 3–4

CyberStacks (1998). Available at http://www.public.iastate.edu/~CYBERSTACKS/

DESIRE (1998) Available at http://www.ukoln.ac.uk/metadata/DESIRE/classification

Dewey for Windows (1998). Dublin, OH: OCLC, 1996. An updated Dewey for Windows Version 1.1 was released in February 1998 and provides an electronic version of DDC 21st edition.

Dodd, D. G. (1996), 'Grass roots cataloguing and classification: food for thought from World Wide Web oriented hierarchical lists', *Library Resources and Technical Services*, **40** (3), 275–86

Electronic Dewey (1993), *Electronic Dewey: DDC20*, Dublin, OH: OCLC.

Ellis, D. (1996), *Progress and Problems in Information Retrieval*, 2nd edn, London: LA Publishing.

Fallows, J. M. (1996), 'Navigating the galaxies', *Atlantic Monthly*, **277** (4), April, 104–7.
Hill, J. (1990), 'Things are taking a little longer than that: a response to Dewey Decimal Classification in the Online Environment', *Cataloging and Classification Quarterly*, **11** (1), 59–69.
Hjorland, B. (1997), *Information Seeking and Subject Representation: an activity-theoretical approach to Information Science*, Westport, CT: Greenwood Press.
HyPursuit Project. (1998), *MIT Computing Science Laboratories*. Available at http://www.prsg.lcs.mit.edu:80/Project/CRS/HyPursuit
Johns, C. (1997), 'Cataloguing Internet resources: an administrator's viewpoint', *Journal of Internet Cataloguing*, **1** (1), 18.
Jul, E. (1997), 'Now that we know the answers, what are the questions?', *Journal of Internet Cataloguing*, **1** (3). Available at http://www.hawthornepressInc.com/jic/jic/nr3–42
KBS Media Lab, (1998). Available at http://delphi.kstr.lth.se/kbs/projects/kbscross.html
Koh, G. S. (1995), 'Options in Classification Available Through Modern Technology', *Cataloguing and Classification Quarterly*, **19** (3/4), 207.
Kowalk, W. (1993), 'The Saarbrucken subject catalogue according to the Eppelsheimer Method in the OPAC', in H.-J. Hermes and L. Havekost. *Die Systematik im OPAC: über das Instrumentarium zum Ordnen und Wiederfinden* (The use of classification systems in OPACS: On the instruments available for ordering and retrieving.), Oldenburg.
Lesk, M. (1997), *Practical Digital Libraries: books, bytes and bucks*, San Francisco: Morgan Kaufman, p. 174.
Levy, D. M. et al. (1995), 'Going Digital: a look at assumptions underlying digital libraries', *Communications of the ACM*, **38** (4), 77–84.
Library of Congress (1994), *Library of Congress Cataloger's Desktop: Windows CD-ROM*, Washington, DC: Library of Congress, Cataloging Distribution Service.
Library of Congress (1996), *Library of Congress Classification Plus CD*, Washington, DC: Library of Congress Cataloguing Distribution Service.
Liu, S. (1990), 'Online classification notation: proposal for a flexible notation system', *International Classification*, **17** (1), 14–20.
Lowry, C. B. (1995), 'Preparing for the Technological Future: a Journey of Discovery', *Library Hi-tech*, **13** (3), 39–53.
Mann, T. (1993), *Library Research Models: a Guide to Classification, Cataloging and Computers*, New York and Oxford: Oxford University Press.
Marcella, R. (1994), *A New Manual of Classification*, Aldershot, UK: Gower.
Marchionini, G. (1995), *Information seeking in electronic environments*, New York and Cambridge: Cambridge University Press (Cambridge Series on Human-Computer Interaction, 9).
Markey, K. and Demeyer, A. H. (1986), *Dewey Decimal Classification Online Project: evaluation of a Library Schedule and Index integrated into the subject searching capability of an online catalog*, Dublin, OH: OCLC.
McFadden, T. G. (1993), 'I wonder who's indexing the Internet now?' in *Proceedings of the 25th Annual Meeting of the American Society of Indexers, Alexandria (VA) May 20–22*, pp. 95–109.
McIlwaine, I. (1995), 'UDC Centenary. The present state and future prospects', *Knowledge Organization*, **22** (2), 64–9.
McKiernan, G. (1995), *Participatory WWW Database Development and Resource Classification*, bit.listserv.asis-1 (13 December).

McKiernan, G. (1997), 'The New/Old World Wide Web order: the application of functionality to facilitate access and use of a WWW database of Science and Technology Internet Resources', *Journal of Internet Cataloguing*, **1**, 48.

McMahon, K. (1995), 'Effective searching of BUBL', *Computers in Libraries*, **15** (1), January, 62–3.

Miksa, F. and Doty, P. (1994), 'Intellectual realities and the digital library', in J. L. Schnase et al., *Proceedings of Digital Libraries '94. College Station, Texas; June 19–21 1994*. Available at http://abgen.cvm.tamu.edu/DL94/paper/miksa.html

Mitchell, J. S. (1998), 'In this age of WWW is classification redundant?', *Catalogue and Index*, **127**, 5.

Mundie, D. (1998), *Organizing computer resources; or, How I learned to stop worrying and love the DDC*. Available at http://ivory.lm.com/~mundie/CyberDewey/organizing_computers.html

Neuminster, S. M. (1997), 'Cataloguing Internet Resources: a practical viewpoint', *Journal of Internet Cataloguing*, **1**, 25–45.

Oddy, P. (1996), *Future Libraries, Future Catalogues*, London: LA Publishing.

Richmond, A. (1998), *The WEB librarian*. Available at http://www/stars/com/WLn/

ROADS (1998). Available at http://ukoln.bath.ac.uk/roads

Shafer, K. (1996), *A brief guide to Scorpion*, Dublin, OH: OCLC. Available at http://orc.rsch.oclc.org:6109/bintro.html

Shearer, J. and Thomas, A. (1997), *Cataloguing and Classification: Trends, Transformation, Teaching and Training*, London: Library Association Publishing.

Signpost (1998). Available at http://www.signpost.org

Steinberg, S. G. (1996), 'Seek and ye shall find (maybe)', *Wired*, May. Available at http://www.hotwired.com/wired/4.05/features/indexweb.html

Super LCCS (1996), *Super LCCS CD*, Detroit: Gale Press.

Svenonius, E. (1983), 'Use of classification in online retrieval', *Library Resources and Technical Services*, **27** (1), 76–80.

Trotter, Ross (1995), 'Electronic Dewey: The CD-ROM version of the Dewey Decimal Classification', in A. R. Thomas (ed.), *Classification. Options and Opportunities*, New York and London: The Haworth Press, pp. 213–34.

van der Walt, M. S. (1998), 'Snuffelgidse op die Web: die gebruik van klassifikasie vir die oranisering van inlingtingsbronne op die Internet', *South African Journal of Librarianship and Information Science*, **66** (2), 56–66.

Vizine-Goetz, D. (1996), 'Using library classification schemes for Internet resources' (position paper), in *Proceedings of the OCLC Internet Cataloguing Colloquium, San Antonia, Texas*, January. (The Internet version is cited at the end of the next chapter.)

Vizine-Goetz, D. (1998), *Online classification: Implications for classifying and document-like object] retrieval*. Available at http://orc.rsch.oclc.org:6109/dvgisko.htm

Wellisch, H. (1981), 'Year's work in subject analysis: 1980', *Library Resources and Technical Services*, **25**, July/September, 295–309.

Will, L. (1997), 'Dewey for Windows 1996', *The Electronic Library*, **15** (3), 194.

Woodward, J. (1996), 'Cataloging and Classifying Information Resources on the Internet', *Annual Review of Information Science and Technology (ARIST)*, **31**, 189–220.

5 Classification and the Internet
Alan MacLennan

This chapter will first describe some of the problems regarding the application of classification schemes to the retrieval of Internet resources, and will discuss briefly search engines and resource catalogues, two currently popular methods of resource identification. It will then move on to consider usage of the well-known universal, and better-known specialized schemes in catalogues and gateway services. Next, it will consider the possibilities of automatic classification techniques using the universal schemes, and will look at two examples. The chapter concludes with a look at some ideas for the future of classification and document retrieval on the Internet.

The problem

In the few years since the Internet has gained prominence in the public consciousness, at least in those countries where the telecommunications infrastructure permits it to be exploited at an acceptable speed and quality, the Information and Library Service (ILS) community has been adjusting to its incredible potential as an information resource.

Full exploitation of this potential is hampered by a number of factors, many of which, such as bandwidth, political, or censorship restrictions, are beyond the scope of ILS work. A major problem in ILS terms arises with the organization of the material 'out there'. If a resource is not organized, is there justification for regarding it as a 'resource' at all, or is the Internet merely, as Lynch (1997) claims, a huge amount of disorganized data, a 'chaotic repository for the collective output of the world's digital "printing presses" '?

The skills in which information workers have traditionally specialized – identification, acquisition, cataloguing and classification of resources –

would seem to be those which have much to offer the organization of Internet resources, but it appears that, to date, these have not been successfully applied to a significant degree.

The salient problem is one of number – a vast number of documents, in many electronic formats, growing daily and numbering many millions at the time of writing. The number of topics with which the documents deal has also increased – one need merely consider the number and variety of Usenet newsgroups, and the constantly simmering 'flame wars' regarding 'off-topic' postings to them. The fact that networking influences so many aspects of life has itself created new subject areas unknown a few years ago. 'Virus contamination by Java applet', a topic which would recently have been without denotation, is currently one on which information is urgently sought. There are documents which deal with such topics, but how is the user to identify them? The means of access to these documents has, broadly, fallen into two categories – use of 'search engines'; and use of 'catalogues', or pages of links.

Search engines

Search engine services are typically commercial ventures, funded by advertising, which use programs (often known as 'spiders' or 'robots') to construct, periodically, indices of resources accessible through the Internet. Such resources are often, though not necessarily, limited to World Wide Web pages, and are accessed by the program's exhaustive following of hypertextual links, beginning with a set of 'seed' Web pages.

The index produced by a 'spider', essentially a large inverted file, is searchable by methods which vary according to the sophistication of the search engine concerned, but will typically include some form of Boolean query, the capacity to do a string search, or the option of limiting the scope of search to document titles.

The fact that each service tends to have a unique search interface makes the transition between different engines more difficult for the user than it might otherwise be. The user is accustomed to monolithic suites of software applications, sharing input conventions. If conventions such as implied Boolean 'AND' were adopted universally, the user would be more free to concentrate on the engine with the database best fitted to the information need.

It is useful to store and access electronically the surrogate for a bibliographic item which is known to be available at a certain location, but when the item is itself an electronic document, the location of which may be changed at any time, or of which multiple copies may be 'mirrored' around the world, then a 'search engine approach' to its retrieval must be aided by its carrying of its information with it. A standard to be used for this purpose has already been suggested: the Dublin Core (DC) Metadata element set was defined as a result of the March 1995 Metadata Workshop, sponsored by the Online Computer Library Center (OCLC) and the National Center for Supercomputing Applications (NCSA). Dublin Core allows for the inclusion of subject scheme and keyword information in the header of a networked document, so that, for example, DDC and LCC classmarks and medical subject headings (MeSH) could all be added to the record.

The means for retrieval of Dublin Core-enhanced records are still at the early stages of development, but this idea of 'metadata' – data about data, which are included with the document itself – provides the possibility of enhancing records, so that they may be identified by future systems. There are also experiments being carried out in the automatic generation of DC information, which move the focus towards the topic of automatic classification.

Catalogues

In WWW terms, as in the more familiar paper-based environment, catalogues range from single-page lists (a 'list of links', for example LibrarySpot (1998)) to complex, hierarchically organized and cross-referenced structures (for example the Librarians' Index to the Internet (Leita, 1998)).

An interesting meta-resource is provided by McKiernan, Science and Technology Reference Librarian and Bibliographer, Science and Technology Services Department, Iowa State University Library. My perspective on this may complement others within this book, for example Robert Newton in Chapter 4. McKiernan (1998) describes his resource, CyberStacks (sm) as 'a centralized, integrated, and unified collection of significant World Wide Web (WWW) and other Internet resources categorized using the Library of Congress Classification (LCC) scheme. Resources are organized under one or more relevant Library of Congress class numbers and an associated publication format and subject description.' This exemplifies the 'catalogue' approach in that it is a human-maintained resource which does not claim to be an exhaustive catalogue, but which points to resources which have been evaluated by the maintainers and found to be worthy of inclusion. The user gets a high degree of relevance, but this is achieved at cost of recall. Although we can perhaps believe that in the comparative infancy of electronic documents, and in a highly specialized subject area, a comprehensive coverage is possible, it must be doubted whether this can be maintained.

In the United Kingdom, BUBL describes its mission as to 'provide value-added access to Internet resources and services of academic, research and professional significance to the U.K. higher education community' (BUBL, 1998). This service, funded by the Joint Information Systems Committee (JISC), researches and receives community-contributed resource descriptions which are evaluated by staff and may be added to the service. Resource descriptions are searchable and subjects can be browsed by alphabetical order or DDC classmark.

Classification schemes

The fact that search engines do not, typically, offer an option to search by classification is indicative of the fact that such information is not commonly included in the source documents. This might be seen as an unwelcome return to the days of traditional library cataloguing, pre-dating the availability of records with suggested classmarks from centralized agencies (such as the British Library or OCLC), or of Cataloguing-in-Publication (CIP) carried out by agencies, using data supplied by publishers. Cataloguing standards developed from the electronic exchange of bibliographic data, such as UKMARC, offer the facility to include subject information often in a variety of forms, for example DDC, LCC and Library of Congress Subject Headings (LCSH). This approach is adequate for a relatively static collection, for example one contained in a single library, or even in a large expanding collection such as that belonging to the member libraries of the OCLC, but cannot usefully be applied to an environment where documents appear in a manner beyond any form of bibliographic control.

DDC and LCC are hierarchical schemes which have notation reflecting the structure of subjects. As such, there seems every probability that they can provide adequate access to adequately classified Internet resources. Vizine-Goetz, in an OCLC Internet Cataloguing Project Colloquium position paper, conducted an analysis of the 50 most popular categories in the popular catalogue Yahoo! (1998), and a comparison with DDC and LCC classmarks revealed that, with a few exceptions (for example the ability to subdivide geographical areas by topic), 'mappings of the other categories indicate that DDC and LCC have sufficiently wide topic coverage for classifying Internet resources' (Vizine-Goetz, 1998). It might be questioned whether this is sufficient for the casual user who is unfamiliar with the classification used, and indeed one of Vizine-Goetz's recommendations is to 'decompose and code class number components to identify the specific subject and aspects represented' (ibid.). Other recommendations are concerned with currency and extension of literary warrant to Internet resources. It may be unrealistic to expect the average user to learn the intricacies of one or more general classification schemes, but if access is supported by adequate indexing, and if links to other classifications and languages are available, as is the case, then it seems that the general schemes have a worthwhile part to play.

Specialized classification systems used include the National Library of Medicine (NLM) classification, used by OMNI (Organising Medical Networked Information, 1998), which specializes in providing access to biomedical information. Here is an example of a specialized area of knowledge, better catered to by a specialized classification than would be possible by using one of the universal schemes. There are similar schemes operating, for example in the field of engineering, at the Edinburgh Engineering Virtual Library (EEVL, 1998a), which uses 'an in-house scheme which is loosely based on the Ei Classification developed by Engineering Information Inc' (EEVL, 1998b); and in computing, where the Association for Computing Machinery's (ACM) Computing Classification Scheme (CCS) is used by Ariadne (Medoc Konsortium, 1998).

There are, of course, many examples of informal, non-traditional classification 'schemes' by which links to resources are organized, a good example being that developed by Yahoo! itself. This scheme stemmed from the personal needs of its founders to keep their links organized and has developed from there. As noted above, LCC and DDC can be mapped onto it with reasonable levels of correspondence, and, given its evident popularity, it must be considered a good example of a 'home-brewed' scheme, though it has no evident notation and might be considered as a subject index. In common with other resources, Yahoo! has added much functionality to its basic structure and these 'catalogues' often now include search engines which operate on their own, or on global databases, links to other specialized services (such as 'people finders') or, recently, interfaces with permit users to research their personal machines' resources and Internet resources simultaneously.

Automatic classification

Here, some personal perspectives may be added to the observations of Robert Newton in Chapter 4. Scorpion is a research project at OCLC (1998), intended to provide 'tools for automatic subject recognition based on well known schemes like the Dewey Decimal System'. It appears, from the published results, to have a good degree of success in assigning relevant Dewey numbers to electronic documents, and, as such, would seem to have potential in assisting human classification of documents. It must, however, be questionable whether its ability to generate a list of suggested classmarks, from which a human classifier can select, is indicative of an eventual capability definitively to assign classmarks to wide-ranging resources.

Scorpion used the principle that a document can be 'treated as a query against a Dewey Decimal System database using ranked retrieval. The results of the search can then be treated as the subjects of the document. Subject assignment in this manner provides clear differentiation from the traditional computer indexing behind the currently available free search services' (Shafer, 1998). It appears that the initial results of this approach have been satisfactory, and work is currently under way to improve results by development of techniques for filtering the initial results from the Scorpion engine (Shafer, Subramanian and Fausey, 1998).

It should also be considered that, as there will inevitably be a loss in precision when assigning classmarks to documents automatically, and a comparable loss in precision when translating search terms into classmarks, the whole process may be so subject to loss or imprecise as to render it useless. It is not suggested that this problem is insurmountable, but that it may not be resolvable in an acceptable timescale. It may well be that before these mappings can be refined sufficiently to be useful a new approach will have emerged which makes them obsolete.

There is a common criticism that the universal schemes are 'ontologically biased'; that is, they impose the world view of their creators; they are insufficiently current; they do not provide sufficient room for expansion; and so on. These criticisms can be partially responded to by faceted classification schemes, but then mnemonic problems arise. However, if we are relying on automated systems to handle the classification for us, running out of numbers becomes less of a problem – we need not restrict the notation to, for example, the letters of the alphabet and the digits 0 to 9, with punctuation marks as indicators. Consider the Domain Name Server (DNS) system, which interprets mnemonic URL requests into the 'dotted-quad' format of the Internet protocol (IP) address 'on the fly'. This operation takes place without the user having to be aware of what is actually going on: it is transparent to the user. DNS machines update each other automatically, so that each has a current picture of the addresses in its area. Such a system could be exploited for resources also, in order that a current 'image' of resources in a particular subject area could be maintained on a central machine, which supplied updates, on request, to client machines responsible for that subject area.

The nature of hypertextual documents leads us into another set of possibilities in cataloguing. For many years documents have been of more than one 'dimension'; that is, one document can refer to others, conventionally by citation. With the implementation of electronic hypertext, in the form of the WWW, this citation adds new dimensions to a document. The citation of a document becomes, in effect, its means of retrieval. The implication is that a single document can become the gateway to numerous other documents.

Where does this leave classification? It would be meaningless or trivial to categorize every document as a 'list of links', yet this is what many potentially valuable documents will essentially be, or what they will at least include. If we can free our idea of a classification as something essentially linear – a classified sequence, supported by a subject and an author/title index, for example – perhaps we could grasp the potential offered to us by computers and make the leap into multidimensional classification.

There has long been the problem in libraries that books can only be organized in a single sequence. Books can only be shelved in classification order, or alphabetically by author, or alphabetically by title, or by colour of cover, or whatever, but only in one way. On the Internet, you do not have to shelve books or tidy the shelves. This frees up time for many other activities, such as contemplating multidimensional classification. Rather than a sequential arrangement, rather than constraining the 'universe of knowledge' into a linear arrangement (no wonder we get cross-classification, where things pop up in more than one place!), what if there was a concept of 'information space'?

The information space need not be limited even in the number of its dimensions – remember that mathematicians (and computers) can work with n-dimensional spaces. The user, or indeed the librarian, does not have to grasp the full detail of how items are 'shelved' in this space, merely to provide the information necessary for retrieval. In 'closed-stack' libraries of the past (largely, but still in national libraries, for example) it does not matter to the user in what order, if any, material is shelved. The operation is, again, 'transparent': you fill out a request slip; you receive an item. Where is the need to know more? If you want to know about items on related subjects, then request an item which has the characteristics of supplying such details. The item you request will be at a position in the information space which indicates that it carries citations to related items.

Three-dimensional 'information spaces' have been represented using Virtual Reality Modelling Language (VRML). This type of representation might depict one's desired document as, for example, a leaf on a branch of a tree in a forest (maintaining a hierarchical analogy), or, perhaps, a stone on a mountain on a continent on a planet orbiting a particular sun. Obviously, this is not a true three-dimensional representation, but, in the same sense that a two-dimensional drawing can suggest a three-dimensional object, a virtually three-dimensional image could be used to suggest representations in more than three dimensions.

A 1997 paper from the United Kingdom Office of Library Networking (UKOLN) describes at some length the use of classification schemes in organizing subject access to Internet resources. The review of automatic classification notes that, 'there are no known examples of traditional library classification being overtaken completely by computer software', but identifies several areas in which established classification systems are used in Internet services. Applications involving WAIS databases may now be of historical interest only, such resources having been superseded by the World Wide Web, although the techniques may still be valid. The Nordic WAIS/WWW project (Ardo and Koch, 1998) at Lund University Library used the technique of gathering sets of words from the description and keyword lists, and subject fields of databases, and comparing the words with the UDC vocabulary. Matches of the vocabulary against the UDC vocabulary led to suggested classifications, weighted according to the area of the database description from which the matching term originated. The final classification was arrived at by comparing the weightings for the different suggested classifications. The authors claim that the classification tool will adapt to classification schemes other than UDC, so perhaps this project, which was 'caught in time' by technological developments, still has the potential to be valuable.

It seems, then, that there can be a place for the use of automated application of universal classification schemes in provision of access to Internet resources. This can be complemented in specific subject areas by the use of specialized schemes, and there should, for some time to come, remain the need for human-constructed and maintained 'gateway' services, organizing evaluated resources according to established practice. Classification as an activity is most likely to remain a decentralized occupation, in keeping with trends in networking. We can imagine that different classification schemes will continue to be adapted to give different perspectives on the global resource, but this will continue to be a retrospective activity – new 'forms' of electronic document appear so frequently, for example, that a form facet of a faceted scheme would have to be kept in constant revision. Finally, it is noted that software is now appearing which claims to reduce time spent online by 'predicting' which page the user is likely to require next and downloading it pre-emptively, while the current page is being read. Currently this apparently 'intelligent' behaviour is accomplished by merely downloading all links from the current page, but might it not be the case that the network itself might be used to spare us the effort of classifying it? Equipping electronic resources with metadata provides them with the best hope of retrieval, not only using the current tools, but also using tools which have not yet been developed.

A final speculation

It might be useful in conclusion to imagine a document which, using software on the server on which it resides, searches the Web for catalogues appropriate to its content, retrieves and updates the catalogue pages to include links to itself, monitors the number of 'hits' on itself originating from these pages and, finally, 'settles down' at the location in each catalogue at which it received the best response. If the catalogue pages had universal permission to write, then this is, effectively, a minimal specification for a 'self-classifying document'. It would require an array attached to each document holding URLs and an associated 'hit-count', plus an expiry date for the evaluation period. All the elements needed for this scenario are already available. It may bring to mind a children's story, in which a poor little library book which has never been borrowed drags itself along the shelves until someone finally notices it, or one of Ranganathan's 5 Laws of Library Science *'every book its reader* . . . [where] the reference librarian has, therefore, to act as a canvassing agent for every document in the library' – but the electronic analogy to that is now a real possibility. Now all that we have to worry about is the user interface with the classification, but that's a whole new story . . .

References

Ardo, A. and Koch, T. (1998), 'Nordic WAIS/World Wide Web Project: Subproject: automatic classification of WAIS database'. Available at http://www.ub2.lu.se/autoclass.html

BUBL Information Service (1998), *BUBL Information Service home page*. Available at http://www.bubl.wc.uk

EEVL (1998a), *EEVL: Edinburgh Engineering Virtual Library*. Available at http://eevl.icbl.hw.ac.uk/

EEVL (1998b), *An EEVL solution to engineering information on the Internet*. Available at http://www.eevl.ac.uk/paper1.html/

Leita, C. (1998), *Librarians' index to the Internet*. Available at http://sunsite.berkeley.edu/InternetIndex/ .

Lynch, C. (1997), 'Searching the Internet', *Scientific American*, **276** (3), 44–8.

McKiernan, G. (1998), *CyberStacks (sm)*. Available at http://www.public.iastate.edu/~CYBERSTACKS/

Medoc Konsortium (1998), *Ariadne: Entrypoint – version 5.0* Available at http://ariadne.inf.fu-berlin.de 8000/

OCLC (Online Computer Library Center) (1998), *The Scorpion Project*. Available at http://orc.rsch.oclc.org:6109/

Organizing Medical Networked Information (1998), *OMNI welcome page*. Available at http://www.omni.ac.uk/

Shafer, K. (1998), *A brief introduction to Scorpion*. Available at http://orc.rsch.oclc.org:6109/

Shafer, K., Subramanian, S. and Fausey, J. (1998), 'Measures for evaluating automatic subject assignment of electronic resources'. Available at http://orc.rsch.oclc.org:6109?bintro.html/

StartSpot Mediaworks (1998), *LibrarySpot: the best of libraries, newspapers, encyclopaedias, maps and more in one spot*. Available at http://www.libraryspot.com/

UKOLN.DESIRE-RE 1004 (1997), *The role of classification schemes in Internet resource description and discovery.* Available at http://www.ukoln.ac.uk/metadata/desire/classification/class_ti.htm/

Vizine-Goetz, D. (1998), 'Using library classification schemes for Internet resources. OCLC Office of Research and Special Projects'. Available at http://www.oclc.org/oclc/man/colloq/v-g.htm

Yahoo Inc. (1998), 'Yahoo' Available at http://www.yahoo.com/

6 The future of faceted classification
A. C. Foskett

As I have set out elsewhere (Foskett, A. C., 1996), a classification scheme consists of four parts: schedules; notation; index; and organization. If we are to consider the future of faceted classification, we must consider each scheme within each of these four constraints, to see whether it has the ability to remain viable into the future, or whether we can take any steps which will guide it into the right direction.

Schedules

The schedules of classes or their components are the key part of any classification, and we see the introduction of what we now know as facet analysis in Dewey's first edition. Dewey must have noted that he enumerated what became known as the 'form divisions' at each main class heading in the Dewey Decimal Classification (DDC), and in the second edition he developed this idea, putting the subdivisions into a separate table, which could be applied as needed throughout the classification. It is also in the first edition that we see clearly the idea that, for example, the subdivisions of literature could apply to literature as a whole, but also to specific languages. A similar approach is found in the Library of Congress Classification (LCC) literature schedules, where the tables show the parallels between the works of one author and another. However, Dewey did not pursue this idea beyond these few rather obvious examples, and it was Ranganathan who first formalized the fact that facet analysis can be applied to any subject, and that the schedules of a classification scheme should reflect this. The idea of facet analysis was further developed by the Classification Research Group (CRG) in the 1950s (Foskett, D. J., 1962). It is perhaps worth mentioning that some thirty years of teaching facet analysis to students, who were required to develop their own (small-scale) scheme, did not reveal any subject which did not lend itself to this treatment. From its success, we must assume that the future of intellectual information retrieval lies in the first place in adequate facet analysis.

At the same time, we must accept the fact that facet analysis has some limitations. It places an inherent restriction on linkages, for example. Links may be superordinate (Broad term–Narrower term), or subordinate (NT–BT), but these must be generic or quasi-generic relationships, a useful distinction first recognized by Austin (1974). Links may be coordinate, dealing with related terms (RT–RT), but these must be restricted to terms within the same facet. The danger of allowing other linkages was illustrated by Coates (1988) with reference to Library of Congress Subject Headings (LCSH), but his comments are valid generally. On the other hand, statistical analysis of text often reveals other linkages (Doszkocs, 1978) which would be excluded by facet analysis. We can also argue that the rigid framework of facet analysis precludes the kind of lateral thinking cited by De Bono (1967) as the source of many significant ideas. Nevertheless, facet analysis does appear to be the most important tool at our disposal for the analysis of subjects and their listing in a classification schedule, and we should expect it to be increasingly important in the future.

A schedule must make provision not only for single concepts but also for composite subjects: not merely Steel (material) and Welding (operation), but also 'The welding of steel'; not merely Drama (literary form), Elizabethan (period applying to English literature) and Allegory (mode or perspective), but also 'A discussion on the use of allegory in post-Elizabethan drama'.

The schedule must therefore not only enumerate individual concepts, but provide the means of combining them as necessary. Unfortunately, we cannot regard this as a 'one-off' operation. Knowledge is not static, and is in fact growing at an exponential rate; new concepts and new combinations arise with distressing frequency. In Colon Classification (CC) Ranganathan put forward the idea of a 'self-perpetuating classification', in which users would all develop the scheme in the same way; practice has shown that he was over-optimistic. The 'seminal mnemonics' which he proposed proved to be of limited value, and certainly did not provide solutions to more than a few situations. The classifier is obliged to look carefully at the literature and determine the structure of concepts within it; new concepts can then be fitted into the same structure. But what if a whole new facet is required, and the structure proves inadequate? This would be very rare, and suggests that analysis was inadequate in the first place, or based on a poor sample of the literature. However, it can be accommodated in a suitable schedule. LCSH can incorporate new headings with no difficulty in its alphabetical arrangement; it is only when we move on to the second feature of a scheme, the notation, that problems arise.

The discussion so far suggests that facet analysis is most effective in a clearly defined subject area (basic class) which can be analysed in detail, and the first schemes devised by the CRG were indeed schemes on this scale. The practice has continued, and new examples appear regularly in the journal literature; we must also not ignore all those that exist but do not make it that far, and are thus known only to those who develop them. A good example of the published type is The Dickens House classification (Harris, 1987). This shows the advantages of being restricted to a clearly defined and well-established subject, and there seems to be no reason why it should not continue to be successful in providing access to this particular collection and, by analogy, others like it.

Having found an answer to the problems of analysis within a particular subject, the CRG turned to the problem of general classification, with funding from a NATO grant. A distinction which has become important is that between a *general* classification, which comprises a set of classifications for specific subjects which between them cover a substantial part of the universe of knowledge, and a *universal* classification, which tries to put its constituent subjects into some kind of logical arrangement (CRG, 1997). The ideas of the CRG have been concentrated on the development of the second edition of the Bibliographic Classification (BC2) into a universal classification, and it is in that scheme that most work has been concentrated in the past twenty years. The scheme is being developed on strictly faceted lines rather than the largely enumerative method used by Bliss himself; however, the main class order is little changed, reflecting the considerable thought given by Bliss to this part of the scheme. Within each subject, the CRG are developing the schedules using additional theoretical approaches such as that of 'integrative levels' put forward by D. J. Foskett as long ago as 1960.

Even with the concentrated approach in the development of BC2, problems still arise. A good example is the schedule for Chemistry: while Inorganic Chemistry remains relatively static, the same is by no means true of Organic Chemistry, and the ability of chemists to synthesize new compounds, together with the enormous effort being put into discovering new natural compounds, means that this is a classic example of an open-ended schedule. So far facet analysis has been successful, but will there be a limit at which it proves to be impossible to cater for future directions? Certainly there will be a need for continuing detailed work based on an adequate knowledge of the literature and of current developments.

A significant factor in this work has been the use of BC2 schedules as the basis for thesauri (Aitchison, 1986), and the possibility that the schedules may be used in schemes such as UDC. Although the scheme is largely an 'amateur' effort, in that the schedules are not being produced for the classification of a large library by a large organization, good progress is being made on many of the theoretical points, which will in turn advance the development of other schemes.

It is worth mentioning the Broad System of Ordering (BSO), which was developed by a small group for UNISIST as a means of classifying *institutions* rather than documents. Despite – or perhaps because of – its small editorial panel, the scheme is now in its fourth revision, available as computer-readable files. This scheme is also developed on faceted principles, though this is not immediately obvious; in order to make it more widely acceptable, the editors omitted much of the facet structure, which is present but implicit, and many potential notes. Although the scheme is now available on a Web site, it is not clear whether it is being widely used – or at all; its support from UNISIST appears to have evaporated, as does that body itself.

The Universal Decimal Classification has always been a *general* classification, in that it has consisted of a large number of separate subject classifications within the framework established in 1894 from the fifth edition of DDC. The only major change to main class order has been the transfer of Philology and Language to a place alongside Literature. There is therefore less concern about inserting new schedules to replace old, the only caveat being that there should not be any clash. In recent times the management of UDC has changed significantly, and one consequence has been the possibility of adopting schedules from BC2, giving them a suitable decimal notation, as discussed in the chapter on UDC (Chapter 8). Future schedules may thus be faceted, though a large number of enumerative schedules remain at present.

Notation

The notation must show the preferred order; this is its primary function. A pure notation will fulfil this function more clearly than any other, and we should therefore expect the future to show ever more emphatically the advantages of this approach. However, a notation must also perform other functions: it must allow the insertion of new concepts within the appropriate facets; it should allow for the insertion of a new facet – though as we have said, this will be very rare; and it must allow for the unambiguous representation of composite subjects while maintaining the preferred order.

It is now well established that hospitality – the ability to accommodate new subjects – and expressiveness – the ability to reflect in the notation the hierarchy of the subjects represented – are mutually exclusive, and that hospitality is the more important. It must at the same time be remembered that hospitality is important *for the classifier*, who is not too concerned if the notation does not reflect the hierarchy; DDC has demonstrated that the layout of the schedules can show the hierarchy quite clearly regardless of the notation. By contrast, expressiveness is an aid *for the user* by showing the structure of the subject – though we should not over-estimate the importance of this; LCC is not at all expressive, but this does not seem to worry users. Guiding is far more important in showing the reader the way around the shelf arrangement, or the layout of a bibliography – but guiding is a neglected art in most libraries.

We should therefore expect to see in the future more emphasis on hospitality, and further attempts to reconcile this with a pure notation. One approach is that adopted by Ranganathan; by making the digit 9 'empty', it could be used to extend the notation indefinitely while preserving expressiveness. Thus 1, 2, ... 8, 91, 92 ... 98, 991, 992 ... 998, 9991 etc. would all be coordinate. CC6 used this device, and also refers to the use of z and Z for the same purpose; for example L is Medicine, and LZ is Pharmacognosy. Dewey also used 9 to extend his schedules, as seen in Engineering, where 629 is Other branches of Engineering, including 629.1 Aerospace Engineering and 629.2 Motor land vehicles (both subdivisions of the inserted heading 629.04 Transportation engineering); they may to those 'in the know' appear to be coordinate with other branches of engineering, but they are clearly not in the right place in the schedule. Their place in the hierarchy is, however, shown by type face and size, and indentation.

CC7 uses the idea extensively – so widely, in fact, that one begins to wonder about the practical implementation. During the 1960s, the College of Librarianship Wales used the faceted classification for library science drawn up for the CRG, but switched to DDC because the junior staff found the shelving too complicated. Any scheme that makes shelf arrangement difficult is likely to suffer the same fate. Ranganathan, a mathematician, found no problems with a mixed notation, but the result in CC7 must surely cause endless problems for those who have to shelve by it, and even for the more experienced reference librarians who use it to follow the subject arrangement. Can we expect readers to follow such a complex system? Ranganathan's own concept of 'user-friendliness', discussed by D. J. Foskett (1992), does not appear to apply to his own scheme's notation as it has now developed.

Further problems arise when we consider the problems of combination. If we are to combine single concepts together, then in order to achieve consistency we must have a predetermined citation order, which we follow at all times. However, we must be able to combine the notation for these concepts unambiguously, which means that the need for facet indicators arises. Ranganathan's original solution was to use the colon, but he soon found the limitations of using only one facet indicator, and in CC4 followed up his own theoretical developments by using several facet indicators: the comma to introduce Personality (after the first Round); the semicolon to introduce Matter; the colon to introduce Energy; the full stop to introduce Place; and the apostrophe to introduce Time. As the scheme grew, so the notation grew more and more complicated to achieve infinite hospitality, so that CC7 (1987) uses upper-case and lower-case letters, numbers, and no fewer than fourteen indicators, including some which cannot easily be written unambiguously, for example →, & and ←. Some letters are not used because of the risk of confusion: i, l and o are avoided, but both 0 and O are used. The fact that these two are in many cases incorrectly set by the printer illustrates the kind of problem that may arise if the search for hospitality leads to the wrong answers.

Dewey used Arabic numerals, as the most widely used ordering system. However, he overlooked the problems which arise when the notation is used not only to arrange the concepts listed in the scheme but also their combinations. In practice he used the zero 0 to introduce the 'form divisions' (standard subdivisions), and later used two, three or very occasionally four zeroes to introduce various facets, maintaining the pure notation. In doing this, Dewey foreshadowed the idea of retroactive notation: the use of the symbols of the notation itself as facet indicators. The advantage of retroactive notation is that it permits the combination of symbols to represent composite subjects while remaining a pure notation, with no symbols from another series. Its disadvantages are that it permits only one predetermined combination order, and it tends to be wasteful of notation. If for example we use 0, 1 and 2 as facet indicators, then the remaining facets, which by the Principle of Inversion are the most important, have only the digits 3, 4 . . . 9 to utilise, which may make the notation unduly long. However, the method has been used in DDC21 for the new schedule for music without causing undue reaction.

Another method is to use letters rather than numbers. This is the solution adopted in BC2, and has so far proved successful. The problem of fixed citation order has been overcome by the use of the hyphen where necessary, though this does make the notation mixed. For example, in Social Welfare Q, QL is Minors, Children, and QMW Handicapped persons – defective hearing. Hearing-defective children would then be QMW L, by simple synthesis within Class Q. If, however, everything on children was to be gathered together for a specific purpose, the citation order would be changed, and the notation would become QL-MW.

The question of citation order is a significant point. Over the years, the viewpoint within a subject may change, so that the primary facet becomes one that was previously secondary. It is essential to have some means of catering for this situation. A recent example is that of the Biological sciences, which has a new schedule ('complete revision') in DDC21. In previous editions, the primary facet has been the Organism (Personality) facet: in this case Plants or Animals. The Process (Energy) facet has been secondary in the citation order. In DDC21 this is reversed, so that the Process facet is now the primary facet, with Organism second. Any scheme which is to survive into the future must be able to incorporate this kind of change, which cannot be foreseen. Thirty years ago a change in facet order in the Biological sciences would have been quite uncalled for, but a precisely similar change was made in the classification for library science used in *Library and Information Science Abstracts*, when the Energy facet (classification, cataloguing and similar activities) was made the primary facet rather than the Personality facet (kind of library). In each case the change reflected the changes seen in the literature and in the demands made by users on the system. We must expect similar changes in the future, and faceted schemes of classification must make provision for them. We may for example have to reconsider the requirement that a schedule requires a fixed combination order, as stated earlier, if this order is subject to change over a period of time.

Changes in a classification scheme, and the consequent changes in its notation, mean that the librarian is faced with the problem of reclassification. Dewey recognized that this would be unwelcome, and in DDC2 announced the principle of integrity of numbers: notation would not be reused with a new meaning. Developments – which were expected to be increasing detail rather than complete restructuring – would be accommodated at the existing headings. Time has shown that this view too is over-optimistic, and several new schedules have been incorporated in DDC. The question that faces the librarian is whether to reclassify or to stay with the old – and progressively out-of-date – schedule. Some librarians (for example Berman, 1980) reject changes – though they imply that they will introduce their own changes as necessary; the majority accept the changes, if perhaps reluctantly, not least because the MARC centralized cataloguing records do use the new notation. D. J. Foskett, as quoted (Satija, 1997), has pointed out that the cost of reclassification is actually not large compared with some of the other costs, such as keeping computers up to date, that librarians accept regularly.

However, a new difficulty must be resolved: does one reclassify the whole collection in the subject area under revision, or does one begin a new sequence from a specific date? Printed bibliographies adopt the latter process on a regular basis, but in computerized databases this may lead to confusion. The ERIC database makes clear in its headings any changes that should be noted in searching, and this seems to solve the problem in the search situation, but it is not necessarily a solution that is valid if we are thinking of *arrangement*.

The UDC policy of 'starvation' may be a solution. In any given subject area, only part of the potential notation would be used; a revision could then be incorporated in the unused notation without any clash. The previous notation would remain unused for a set period – in UDC, this was ten years – by which time most of the material classified at that point would have been discarded, and the notation could be used for a further revision if necessary. The idea was neatly used in the revision of DDC21, where 376 Education of Women and 377 Religious education have been left vacant; they could be used for a quite different purpose in a future edition. A more specific example is found in the Biological sciences. In previous editions, most of the foci in the Process facet were in 574; in DDC21, 574 is not used, and the Energy facet is spread throughout the rest of 570, substantially reducing the likelihood of clashes. This particular example may have been fortuitous, but it does illustrate the point: there is a real clash between the inertia of shelf arrangement and the fluidity of knowledge. Any classification scheme for the future must be able to accommodate changing knowledge as represented in documents, but it must also maintain a degree of stability for the classifier, and also for the user, who – as Maurice Line (1988) has frequently pointed out – should not be entirely overlooked.

We should also not overlook the possibility of computer notation. The problems that arise with the inertia of notation only apply when it is used to arrange *things*: books on shelves or entries in a bibliography. If the scheme is to be used as a *thesaurus*, the notation can be used to show relationships within the scheme to aid the classifier/indexer, *but does not appear in its use*. An excellent example is the Art and Architecture Thesaurus (Petersen, 1994) which is based on a faceted classification. Within the facets, each focus is given notation which shows its place in the hierarchy, but this notation is purely to arrange the items and is not shown when the scheme is used in its normal form as a thesaurus. There are numerous changes in the notation from the first edition to the second, but these are immaterial for the user. The PRECIS SIN and RIN files also used notation, allocated at random by computer, to facilitate the cross-reference structure and the reuse of strings, but this was quite invisible to the user (Austin, 1974).

Index

The index to a classification scheme is the *entry* vocabulary: the words that a user will look for when trying to find a subject in the classified arrangement. If the scheme is logical – and a faceted scheme should surely be logical – it should be possible to find one's way to a heading by using the classified arrangement itself. This is the purpose of the Summaries in DDC; using these, it should be possible to get to at least the three-digit number which contains the subject sought. Further explanatory notes within the schedules are intended to make the task of getting to the specific place as easy as possible. Despite all this, the easiest way to get to a specific topic is to look it up in the index – but which index? Are we referring to the index which is an integral part of the scheme, or are we thinking of an index to the actual *use* of the scheme in a particular environment? The latter will of course include all the composite subjects that have been created in the application of the scheme, but will not include any of the individual concepts which have not been used in that application.

A chain index to a faceted scheme can be generated very simply by the use of a computer, using the text which forms the schedules. Such a program has been used in the production of BC2 schedules and their associated indexes, and has been adapted to generate an index to BSO.

However, we must be cautious about such a mechanical approach. Both UDC and DDC have been criticized for their indexes to certain editions, and this has had to lead to the production of a revised index. The schedules do not normally contain all the synonyms which may occur in practice, and these must be added by someone skilled in the subject and its literature. For example, the index to the English Medium Edition of UDC BS1000M 1985 was computer-produced and appeared in 1988; the editors felt constrained to apologize for the quality, and the index to the second edition BS1000M 1994 was produced from computer printout by people skilled in indexing, and is generally regarded as a great improvement. The index to DDC is now produced from the software used to maintain the schedules, but again careful editing is needed to ensure that it is at the high level expected. New synonyms or near-synonyms arise; popular usage changes. It seems unlikely that any scheme in the future, no matter how carefully produced, will be able to rely wholly on a computer-produced index.

Organization

Schemes which are produced without an adequate organization to ensure their continuation are doomed to disaster. One of the major problems with a classification scheme is keeping it up to date, and unless there is some continuing organization to do this, the scheme will eventually wither away, as did Brown's *Subject Classification*. BC has been rescued by a group of devoted librarians (the word is not too strong) under the leadership of Mills, but still faces severe problems; much of it remains to be completed and published, and then the scheme has to be adopted by enough libraries to make its continuation viable. The scheme has probably been the most deeply investigated at the theoretical level, but this remains to be put into practice.

The use of computers to produce MARC records has caused major changes in the area of cataloguing and classification. Many libraries now obtain their cataloguing either directly from the British Library or Library of Congress or through a commercial centre such as OCLC (Online Computer Library Center), and schemes which appear in the MARC records, that is LCC and DDC, have a great advantage. DDC is now part of OCLC, and is linked to the OCLC database of cataloguing records to facilitate its use. It is available in machine-readable form for PCs with Windows, and the printed volumes are models of their kind. LCC is used to arrange the collections of the Library of Congress, and we have their assurance that its production will be continued even if they change their procedures to use it only in the Reading Room collections and arrange their stacks by some other method. Both of these schemes appear certain to continue successfully in the future, and it is apparent that DDC is slowly becoming more firmly based on faceted classification.

What of other schemes? UDC is used by large numbers of European special libraries (including the UK), and the demand may well be sufficient for it to continue now that the management problems which caused so much trouble in the past seem to have been resolved. The proposal to use faceted schedules developed for BC2 should lead to a scheme which is wholly faceted at some time in the future; many users find little or no difficulty in using faceted schedules, so the scheme is likely to continue well used in the future. The special libraries that are its main users do not usually get their cataloguing from the MARC records, which inevitably exclude much of the material of use to them, so this will not be a serious factor.

CC is widely used in India, but is becoming complex and difficult to use. Even Satija (1997) in his review of CC7 casts doubt on the ability of the Documentation Research and Training Institute (DRTC) to maintain the scheme adequately. Satija points out that DRTC is a relatively small special library, and does not have the connection with a large collection which is essential if a scheme is to keep in touch with the literature that is its base.

BC2 and BSO seem less assured of a role. BC2 has adherents, particularly in education libraries in the UK, but finance has always been a problem; although some of the schedules have been sold to form the basis of thesauri, the scheme is not supported by any large library with the financial status to bear the cost of completing the scheme and publishing the schedules. The individuals involved in BC2 and the CRG are not going to continue with their work indefinitely, and many of the new generation think that classification is no longer of great significance: the computer will solve all our retrieval problems.

Is this indeed the case? Will the use of computers in information retrieval make the work of classification redundant? Other chapters deal specifically with technological issues, but some comment specifically in the context of facet analysis may be helpful. At present, computers deal with works in one particular language. English (or Russian, or Japanese); do we need to worry about the half of the world's literature *not* in English? Such a view seems short-sighted. UDC and DDC have both appeared in several languages, and the advantage of notation in not being language-based means that such a scheme can be used as a switching language, moving from the schedules in one language to those in another via the notation. The BSI ROOT Thesaurus (BSI, 1988) has shown that a multilingual thesaurus is feasible – *if* the relationships are shown by symbols rather than letters. (Facet analysis is used in the construction of this thesaurus also.) We still have some way to go before the computer can retrieve information regardless of language.

One thing that the computer can do is search for particular concepts regardless of citation order; we could then use a faceted classification for arrangement while using a parallel computer-based file for more flexible searching. While we choose a citation order with care, we have to accept that it will not suit all of the people all of the time; it is essentially a majority verdict. A computer may enable us to serve everybody equally.

But organizing principles are still required. And in faceted classification we have a simple and consistent method for the analysis of subjects, devised for the arrangement and retrieval of subject information; we would be foolish to neglect it.

References

Aitchison, J. (1986), 'A classification as a source for a thesaurus: the Bibliographic Classification of H.E. Bliss as a source of thesaurus terms and structure', *Journal of Documentation*, **42** (3), 161–81.

Austin, D. (1974), *PRECIS: a manual of concept analysis and subject indexing*, London: British National Bibliography.

Berman, S. (1980), 'DDC19: an indictment', *Library Journal*, **105** (1), 585–9.

BSI (1988), *BSI ROOT Thesaurus*, 3rd edn, Milton Keynes: British Standards Institution.

Coates, E. J. (1988), *Subject Catalogues: headings and structure*, reprinted with new introduction, 1960, London: LAPL.

CRG (1997), 'Minutes of the Classification Research Group', 11 July 1997.

De Bono, E. (1967), *The Use of Lateral Thinking*, London: Cape. (De Bono has pursued the idea in several other books.)

Doszkocs, T. E. (1978), 'An associative interactive dictionary for online searching', *Online Review*, **2** (2), 163–73.

Foskett, A. C. (1996), *The Subject Approach to Information*, 5th edn, London: LAPL.

Foskett, D. J. (1962), 'Thoughts on revising a bibliographic classification scheme', *International Forum on Information and Documentation*, **14** (1), 3–7.

Foskett, D. J. (1992), 'Ranganathan and "User-Friendliness"', *Libri*, **42** (3), 227–34.

Harris, K. (1987), 'A faceted classification for special literature collections', *International Library Review*, **19** (4), 335–44.

Line, M. B. (1988), *Lines of Thought: selected papers of Maurice B. Line*, edited by L. J. Anthony, London: Clive Bingley. Line stresses the importance of not overlooking the user in several of his papers.

Petersen, Toni (ed.) (1994). *Art and Architecture Thesaurus*, 2nd edn, New York: Oxford University Press.

Satija, M. P. (1997), 'The revision and future of Colon Classification', *Knowledge Organization*, **24** (1), 18–23.

7 The Dewey Decimal Classification in the twenty-first century
Joan S. Mitchell

Today, the Dewey Decimal Classification is the world's most widely used library classification scheme. We arrive in the present century with the goal of having the Classification evolve to be the world's most widely used general knowledge organization tool. To realize this vision, efforts are under way on several fronts to improve the Classification for current and future uses. These efforts include: continuous updating to keep pace with knowledge; support of classifier productivity; development of meaningful notation; expanded international use; provision of flexible structures; and ongoing research. This chapter will discuss these efforts through the policies and projects that illustrate how the Dewey Decimal Classification is preparing to be the general knowledge organization tool for the twenty-first century.

Background

In the last decade or so of the twentieth century, the Dewey Decimal Classification has changed its basic format from print to print and electronic, has changed editors, has changed ownership, and has changed development systems. The Dewey Decimal Classification is published in two editions, full and abridged. The latest full print edition, Edition 21, was published in summer 1996 and the latest abridged edition, Abridged Edition 13, was published the following year. Since 1993, the full edition of the Classification has also been published in electronic form. Electronic Dewey, an MS-DOS version of Edition 20, was introduced in 1993 and updated in March 1994. Dewey for Windows, the Microsoft Windows-based CD-ROM version of Edition 21, was released shortly after the publication of Edition 21. An update disc is issued annually.

The Classification is developed and maintained in the Dewey editorial office in the Decimal Classification Division at the Library of Congress (LC). The editorial office has been located at the Library of Congress since 1923, and the application of Dewey numbers to LC bibliographic records has been in place since 1930. The location of the editorial operations in the same department where over 115 000 Dewey numbers are assigned to titles annually means that the editors are close to trends in the literature.

The DDC is developed and updated by the editor and three assistant editors. The editor of Edition 20 and Abridged Edition 12, John Comaromi, died in 1991. In 1993, I became editor as an employee of OCLC Forest Press. The three assistant editors are Library of Congress employees, but all editorial operations are funded by OCLC Forest Press.

Editorial work on the last two full and abridged editions of Dewey has been done using a UNIX-based flat file database system first developed by Inforonics in the late 1980s for the production of Edition 20, and updated by Inforonics for the production of Edition 21 (Beall, 1992). OCLC is developing a new editorial support system based on a new relational database model. Among the features of the new system is an authority control module that will permit the linking of Dewey with other thesauri (Mitchell, 1997).

In 1988, Forest Press, then a division of the Lake Placid Education Foundation, was purchased by OCLC (Online Computer Library Center). OCLC's ownership has resulted in several benefits, the most notable being the strengthened ties between the editorial operations and OCLC Research. OCLC Research developed Electronic Dewey and the prototype for Dewey for Windows. OCLC Research is also involved in projects on automatic vocabulary enhancement, machine-assisted classification, and the development of browsers based on the DDC. These projects will be described later in this chapter.

Changes to the Classification are reviewed by the Decimal Classification Editorial Policy Committee (EPC), a ten-member international board whose main function is to represent the interests of DDC users in advising Forest Press on matters relating to the Classification. EPC is a joint committee of OCLC Forest Press and the American Library Association (ALA), and includes official representatives of OCLC Forest Press, ALA, the Library of Congress and the (British) Library Association.

Updating mechanisms

If the Dewey Decimal Classification aspires to continue to serve its present users and to enjoy wider use as a general knowledge organization tool, then its basic structure and detailed developments must be kept up to date.

We employ a number of long-term and short-term approaches to updating. We often use the vehicle of a new edition to introduce major updates or structural changes. We also provide regular updates through the Dewey home page (http://www.oclc.org/fp/) and Dewey for Windows.

We look at major changes in a field from the viewpoint of 'innovation versus stability' (New, 1996). New observes:

> First we must organize according to enduring principles, then we must keep the general outlines and most of the landmarks of the system recognizable over time. If we do not change at all, we fail in competition for new customers, and eventually lose our old ones. If we change too fast, we risk losing old customers in an effort to win new ones, and we may fail to win new ones if we look too reckless in our innovations.

Major structural changes are undertaken after approval of the proposal by EPC. An initial draft is prepared for EPC approval for distribution to outside reviewers. After comments are received, the draft is refined and a new draft is prepared for EPC review and approval. This process may take a short period of time, as in the case of the upcoming revision of the area table for the United Kingdom, which will be developed and published within a year, or may take more than two decades, which was the case for the major revision of the life sciences in Edition 21.[1]

Edition 21 contains three major revisions: public administration, education, and life sciences. The revision of the public administration schedule was undertaken to improve the structure, reduce US bias, and reverse the citation order from jurisdiction/topic to topic/jurisdiction. The last reflects the shift in the literature of the discipline away from jurisdiction to topic as the central emphasis.

In the revision of 370 Education, two entire sections, 376 Education of women and 377 Schools and religion, have been relocated to subdivisions of 371 Schools and their activities. These relocations reflect the current view in the field of education that each of these topics is an aspect of a broader topic (that is, kind of student and type of school, respectively) rather than a central division of education.

The third major revision, 560–590 Life sciences, includes two complete revisions (570 and 583) and extensive revisions in other areas. The 570 schedule features a reversal in citation order from organism/process to process/organism that in turn addresses a fundamental shift in the discipline away from a focus on organism to a focus on internal biological process.

Edition 21 includes revisions in other disciplines, accommodates new topics, and contains changes to address cultural, social, and political issues. For example, in Edition 21, we have initiated a multi-edition plan to further reduce Christian bias in 200 Religion. We have relocated comprehensive works on Christianity from 200 Religion (where they were equated with the whole of religion) to 230 Christianity, and have relocated the standard subdivisions of Christianity from 201–209 to the appropriate numbers in 230–270 (the Christianity schedule). We have also revised and expanded the schedules for two major religions, 296 Judaism and 297 Islam.

We expect to publish the next full edition of the Classification in 2003. We are investigating major updates in computer science and medicine, continued changes in religion, and other updates as needed. We are exploring ways of simplifying number building in literature, an area in which classifiers are often daunted by the complexity of the instructions. We are also considering the deletion of Table 7 (Groups of persons) because most of the notation is already available in Table 1 and in the schedules 001–999.

We do not wait for a new edition to deliver changes to our users. We keep the Classification up to date on a continuous basis through several devices: two annual publications, *Decimal Classification Additions, Notes and Decisions (DC&)*[2] and the update disc for Dewey for Windows; monthly postings on the Dewey home page of new and changed entries; bi-weekly postings of new LC subject headings mapped to candidate DDC numbers; and occasional postings of application advice.

We issued major revisions of the area table for the United Kingdom and South Africa in late 1998. These changes appeared in *DC&* on the Dewey home page and in the updated database on Dewey for Windows. OCLC Forest Press is considering a biennial publication of the area table that would include these changes and others. In addition to providing an up-to-date resource for Dewey users, the proposed publication might also serve the area notation needs of UDC users, and enjoy general use as a geographic thesaurus.

The new and changed entries that are posted on the Dewey home page on a monthly basis are an example of how Dewey has evolved to meet the needs of our users. We realized after the publication of Edition 21 that annual updates were no longer sufficient to keep pace with knowledge. New and changed entries are posted on the Dewey home page once a month on the first of the month, and are implemented at the Library of Congress upon posting. This process began in July 1997 with the announcement of the new and changed entries for the transfer of Hong Kong from the United Kingdom to China. These new and changed entries are cumulated along with other changes, and published once a year in *DC&* and in the updated database on Dewey for Windows.

We are linking new topics of interest to the DDC using issues of the LC Subject Headings Weekly Lists as a guide. Each week, we download the latest list, select topics of interest, and suggest candidate DDC numbers. We then post the headings and numbers to the Dewey home page on a bi-weekly basis. This process is a method of linking new topics to Classification and a way to provide classifiers with advice on potential numbers for emerging topics. Examples of recent linked headings include Charter schools, Internet addiction, Knowledge management, Media literacy, Perimenopause, Sexism in higher education, Wearable computers, and Webcasting.

We have also posted occasional notes providing application advice – for example, how to classify new and emerging topics in computer science.

In addition to keeping the Classification up to date, these measures contribute to classifier productivity. Our main tool for supporting classifier productivity is Dewey for Windows.

Classifier productivity: Dewey for Windows

Dewey for Windows contains the schedules, tables, Relative Index, Manual, introduction, and glossary of DDC. Additional features include explicit display of hierarchies, sample bibliographic records derived from WorldCat (the OCLC Online Union Catalog), additional index terms, segmentation marks and notes, and selected LC subject headings. The latest update contains several new features designed to enhance classifier productivity.

The electronic edition of the DDC is not encumbered by the same size limitations as the print edition. We are able to add more terms to the electronic index to improve access to the records. For example, the ecology of tundras is indexed as 'Tundras–ecology' in the print edition, and additionally as 'Tundra ecology' in the electronic edition.

Dewey for Windows includes the segmentation marks used by the Library of Congress to show the end of an abridged number or the beginning of a standard subdivision, along with the special segmentation instruction notes. These segmentation marks and instructions permit our cataloguing partners to segment numbers in the same way as the Library of Congress, and provide individual libraries with hints on logical abridgement.

Dewey for Windows contains selected LC subject headings statistically mapped from WorldCat and headings mapped directly by the editors. In Electronic Dewey, the DOS-based CD-ROM version of Edition 20, the subject headings were only statistically mapped, and were limited to subfield a of the 650 field (the USMARC field for LC topical subject headings). In Dewey for Windows, the statistically mapped headings encompass all 6XX LC subject fields and subfields. When we derived the statistical mappings of LC subject headings to Edition 21 numbers, WorldCat did not contain any examples of records classified under the new or changed numbers in the major revisions. Therefore, the editors mapped selected LC subject headings to Edition 21 numbers in the major revisions and entered these into the Dewey database.

Dewey for Windows Version 1.1, the first update disc, includes database updates plus several new features designed to enhance classifier productivity. The database updates include the first issue of *DC&*, selected LCSH/DDC mappings from the home page, and additional built numbers. With the help of OCLC Research, we have identified the 1000 most frequently used built (synthesized) numbers in WorldCat and have added 90 per cent of these to the Dewey for Windows index, along with over 1500 new index terms. The addition of these numbers to the database helps verification of copy cataloguing, and removes the need for classifiers to build the most frequently used synthesized numbers. We plan to continue adding built numbers to the electronic index, especially ones from areas of the schedules in which classifiers find the number building difficult due to the content of the materials to be classified (for example, computer science, music) or to the complexity of the instructions (for example, literature).

One of the new features on the Dewey for Windows update disc is a routine to produce Cutter numbers. We are supplying the OCLC Four-Figure Cutter Tables based on Cutter Three-Figure and Cutter-Sanborn Three-Figure Tables (O'Neill et al., 1997) along with a function that delivers a Cutter number upon input of the main entry or other data on which the Cutter number should be based. There is also a project under way at OCLC to provide book numbers for all Dewey numbers in WorldCat, and to Cutter new entries automatically as they are added to WorldCat.

Dewey for Windows also includes a subscription option for the LC Subject Headings Authority File to be bundled with Dewey for Windows on the same disc.

Julianne Beall, assistant editor of the DDC, has written *Dewey for Windows Guide*, an online companion guide to help classifiers use Dewey for Windows effectively. The guide is included on the Dewey for Windows update disc, and is also available in print (Beall, 1998).

Meaningful notation

One of Dewey's strengths lies in its meaningful notation. During the Dewey Centennial in 1975, Margaret Cockshutt (1976) recounted the historical and emerging roles of meaningful notation in the first 18 editions of the DDC in terms of facets, facet indicators, citation order, and number building. In recent editions, the use of facets and facet indicators has been a recurring feature of major revisions. The 780 Music schedule introduced in Edition

20 is highly faceted, and features a retroactive citation order (Chan et al. 1996, p. 87):

Rock groups 782.421660922

782.42	Songs
1	Facet indicator for general principles (from table under 782.1–782.4)
66	Rock music (from 781.66 Rock)
0922	Collected persons treatment (from Table 1–0922)

The new public administration and life sciences schedules introduced in Edition 21 both make extensive use of facet indicators and notational synthesis. The following example illustrates the usefulness of facet indicators and standard notation:

Digestive processes in the lion 573.319757

573.3	Digestion
1	Facet indicator for specific animal (from 571.1 Animals)
9757	Number following 59 in 599.757 Lion

The facet indicator 1 links the specific physiological process 'digestion' to treatment in a specific animal 'lion', and introduces the notation for the specific animal.

By using uniform notation to represent lions across the Classification, we are able to retrieve lions in the sense of mammals and not in the sense of the international service club:

Lions	599.757
big game hunting	799.27757
conservation technology	639.979757
resource technology	333.959757

and not

Lions International	369.5

The editorial group, EPC, and OCLC Forest Press are committed to the development of meaningful notation and consistent facet indicators whenever practicable. In the short term, the mnemonics of meaningful notation aids classifier productivity; in the long term, meaningful notation provides a powerful subject retrieval device. Several years ago, Songqiao Liu (1993) demonstrated the feasibility of 'decomposing' Dewey numbers in the 700s into their component parts. OCLC Research has recently embarked on a project to address decomposition across the Classification.

World-wide use

What accounts for Dewey's enduring and growing popularity around the globe? The DDC is built on sound principles that make it ideal as a general knowledge organization tool: meaningful notation in universally recognized Arabic numerals, well-defined categories, well-developed hierarchies, and a rich network of relationships among topics. In addition to continuous updating and the efforts towards reduction in US and Christian bias, several other factors contribute to the DDC's ongoing and growing international use: national libraries, national bibliographies, and libraries of every type apply Dewey numbers on a daily basis and share these numbers through a variety of means (including WorldCat); OCLC Forest Press has a vigorous translations programme; and the DDC includes optional arrangements to provide for special needs not served by the standard arrangement.

One of Dewey's great strengths is that the system is developed and maintained in a national bibliographic agency, the Library of Congress. Dewey is used in the national bibliographies of 59 countries: 17 countries in Africa, 13 countries in the Americas/Caribbean region, 7 countries in Europe,[3] 7 countries in the Middle East, and 15 countries in the Asia–Pacific region (Bell, 1997). In addition, EPC, the Dewey review committee described in the first section of the chapter, is international in nature: it is currently chaired by David Balatti, National Library of Canada, and includes a representative from the (British) Library Association and a Forest Press appointee from the Australian Library Association.

OCLC Forest Press is pursuing a vigorous translations programme for the Classification and related materials. In the last decade, the Dewey Decimal Classification has been translated into Arabic, French, Italian, Persian, Spanish, and Turkish. New translations are proposed or under way in Arabic, Chinese, French, Greek, Hebrew, Icelandic, Italian, Norwegian, Russian and Spanish.

Elaine Svenonius (1983) noted Dewey's great potential as a multilingual switching language. At the time of her paper, a machine-readable copy of the Classification was not available, and a communications format that would permit linking between versions had not yet been developed. Dewey's availability in machine-readable form has already been described. Most of the recent translations of the DDC have been prepared with database and/or word processing support.

The USMARC Format for Classification Data was published in 1991. In 1997, several extensions to this were approved as a result of a Library of

Congress proposal based on the recommendations of the IFLA Joint Working Group on a Classification Format (Library of Congress, 1996). The extensions accommodate the data needed to link translations of classification systems with their standard edition. The Permanent UNIMARC Committee has recently appointed a working group to develop a UNIMARC classification format based on the USMARC format. The availability of compatible formats for classification data in USMARC and UNIMARC will permit the representation of Dewey in either format, and the linking between representations of the Classification.

Flexible structures

A knowledge organization system such as Dewey that aspires to be the general knowledge organization tool and to enjoy world-wide usage must offer flexible structures to meet current and future needs. The Dewey Decimal Classification includes optional arrangements to give emphasis to an aspect in a library's collection not given preferred treatment in the standard notation. Options help accommodate cultural differences in the Classification, and provide a mechanism for emphasizing topics of local importance. They are used to provide jurisdictional emphasis; racial, ethnic, national group emphasis; language emphasis; topical emphasis; or emphasis by some other special characteristic (Mitchell, 1995). For example, the National Library of Canada uses C810 for Canadian literature in English and C840 for Canadian literature in French. Edition 21 includes two new optional arrangements for books of Tanakh, the Jewish Bible. The optional arrangements for Tanakh are an example of an alternative structure that meets the needs of users not served by the standard arrangement.

The mapping of other thesauri to the Classification makes it possible to introduce virtual flexible structures in the DDC. Dewey for Windows now contains selected LC subject headings that may be browsed in a separate index. There is no reason why a thesaurus could not be fully mapped to the Classification to extend the vocabulary in the system, and to provide an alternative structure or view. In addition to LCSH and Sears, the editorial group is considering the mapping of Medical Subject Headings (MeSH) and the Thesaurus of ERIC Descriptors for the aforementioned purposes.

Iyer and Giguere (1995) have proposed mapping the American Mathematical Society Mathematics Subject Classification to extend the vocabulary in the system, and to provide a different 'view' of mathematics for the mathematics community. Olson and Ward (1997) at the University of Alberta are working on a project called Fem/DDC that will link A Women's Thesaurus with Dewey to enrich the entry vocabulary and to provide a new view of the Classification to accommodate the interdisciplinary field of women's studies. Cochrane and Johnson (1996) have proposed an alternative view of the Classification in the form of a Dewey hypertextual browser that employs modified DDC captions and the underlying DDC structure without explicit display of the notation.

Research

There is some exciting work going on right now to extend the use of Dewey as a general knowledge organization and navigation tool. Several libraries and Internet information services have independently adopted the Dewey summaries as a way to organize and navigate resources on the World Wide Web. The Dewey home page contains links to some of these systems.

A Dewey-based browser has been developed for NetFirst, OCLC's database of Internet-accessible resources (Vizine-Goetz, 1997a, 1997b). A project began in spring 1998 to 'translate' the Dewey summaries and selected narrower categories into end-user language to make the captions more useful in applications such as Internet browsers.

Several other projects are under way at OCLC Research to prepare Dewey to meet future challenges. Diane Vizine-Goetz (1997a, 1997b) is working on the automatic mapping of LCSH terms to the DDC. Jean Godby (1997) is mapping emerging terminology derived from electronic newspaper abstracts to the DDC. The Scorpion project is an effort to index electronic resources using a Dewey database enhanced with SMART retrieval software (Shafer, 1997). Documents are run against the database as queries, and the results are presented as a ranked list of Dewey numbers.

The future

What has been said above provides indicators of likely progress. Finally, a brief point may be made concerning liaison with other systems and with new generations of technological providers or users. In her chapter on the Universal Decimal Classification in this volume (Chapter 8), Ia McIlwaine has described some potential areas of cooperation between the DDC and the UDC. There is a more general level of cooperation to which all library classification systems must subscribe if they are to flourish as knowledge organization tools in the future: we must educate people inside and outside our profession on the benefits of meaningful notation that provides context and relationships for topics within and across hierarchies.

Notes

1 For a history of the development of this revision, see New (1996).
2 *Decimal Classification Additions, Notes and Decisions (DC&)* will switch to electronic publication on the Dewey home page with vol. 6, no. 2.
3 After the statistics in Bell (1997) were compiled, France began using the DDC in its national bibliography.

References

Beall, Julianne (1992), 'Editing the Dewey Decimal Classification online: the evolution of the DDC database', in Rebecca S. Green (ed.), *Classification Research for Knowledge Representation and Organization; proceedings of the 5th international study conference on classification research, Toronto, Canada, 24–28 June 1991*, pp. 29–37. London and New York: Elsevier.
—— (1998), *Dewey for Windows Guide: Records, Searching, and Number Building*, Albany, NY: OCLC Forest Press. Also available on Dewey for Windows Version 1.1, and at http://www.oclc.org/fp/
Bell, Barbara L. (1997), 'The Dewey Decimal Classification system in national bibliographies', in Lois Mai Chan and Joan S. Mitchell (eds), *Dewey Decimal Classification: Edition 21 and International Perspectives: Papers from a workshop presented at the general conference of the International Federation of Library Associations and Institutions (IFLA), Beijing, China, 29 August 1996*, pp. 43–58. Albany, NY: OCLC Forest Press.
Chan, Lois Mai et al. (1996), *Dewey Decimal Classification: A Practical Guide*, 2nd edn, Albany, NY: OCLC Forest Press.
Cochrane, Pauline, and Johnson, Eric (1996), 'Visual Dewey: DDC in a hypertextual browser for the library user', in Rebecca Green (ed.), *Knowledge Organization and Change: Proceedings of the 4th international ISKO conference, 15–18 July 1996, Washington, D.C.*, pp. 95–106, Frankfurt am Main: INDEKS Verlag.
Cockshutt, Margaret (1976), 'Dewey today: an analysis of recent editions', in Kathryn Luther Henderson (ed.), *Major Classification Systems: the Dewey centennial*, pp. 32–46. Urbana-Champaign, IL: University of Illinois Graduate School of Library Science.
Dewey, Melvil (1996), *Dewey Decimal Classification and Relative Index*. Ed. 21, edited by Joan S. Mitchell, Julianne Beall, Winton E. Matthews, Jr, and Gregory R. New. 4 vols, Albany, NY: OCLC Forest Press.
Dewey for Windows, Version 1.00, Dublin, OH: OCLC Forest Press.
Dewey for Windows, Version 1.1, Dublin, OH: OCLC Forest Press.
Electronic Dewey, Version 1.01, Dublin, OH: OCLC Forest Press.
Godby, C. Jean (1997), 'Enhancing the indexing vocabulary of the Dewey Decimal Classification', *Annual Review of OCLC Research 1996*; pp. 30–33. Also available at http://www.purl.org/oclc/review1996
Iyer, Hemalata and Giguere, Mark (1995), 'Towards designing an expert system to map mathematics classificatory structures', *Knowledge Organization*, 25 (3/4), 141–7.
Library of Congress. Network Development and MARC Standards Office (1991), *USMARC Format for Classification Data; including guidelines for content designation*, Washington, DC: Library of Congress Cataloging Distribution Service, 1991–.
—— (1993), *USMARC Format for Authority Data; including guidelines for content*

designation, Washington, DC: Library of Congress Cataloging Distribution Service, 1993–.

—— (1996), *Proposal no. 97-5, Changes to the USMARC classification format for multilingual classification schemes*. Available from gopher://marvel.loc.gov:70/00/.listarch/usmarc/97-5.cov, and gopher://marvel.loc.gov:70/00/.listarch/usmarc/97-5.doc

Liu, Songqiao (1993), *The automatic decomposition of DDC synthesized numbers*, Ph.D. diss., University of California, Los Angeles.

Mitchell, Joan S. (1995), 'Options in the Dewey Decimal Classification system', *Cataloging & Classification Quarterly*, 19 (3/4), 89–103. Also published in *Classification: Options and opportunities*, edited by Alan R. Thomas, pp. 89–103, New York and London: Haworth.

—— (1997), 'Challenges facing classification systems: A Dewey case study', in *Knowledge Organization for Information Retrieval: Proceedings of the 6th international study conference on classification research, 16–18 June 1997, University College London*, pp. 85–9, The Hague: International Federation for Information and Documentation.

New, Gregory R. (1996), 'Revision and stability in Dewey 21: the life sciences catch up', in Rebecca Green (ed.), *Knowledge Organization and Change: Proceedings of the 4th international ISKO conference, 15–18 July 1996, Washington, D.C.*, pp. 386–95, Frankfurt am Main: INDEKS Verlag.

Olson, Hope A. and Ward, Dennis B. (1997), 'Feminist locales in Dewey's landscape: mapping a marginalized knowledge domain', in *Knowledge Organization for Information Retrieval: Proceedings of the 6th international study conference on classification research, 16–18 June 1997, University College London*, pp. 129–33, The Hague: International Federation for Information and Documentation.

O'Neill, Edward T. et al. (1997), 'Four-figure Cutter tables', *Annual Review of OCLC Research 1996*, pp. 1–18. Also available at: http://www.purl.org/oclc/review1996

Shafer, Keith (1997), 'Scorpion helps catalog the web', *Bulletin of the American Society for Information Science* (October/November), 28–9.

Svenonius, Elaine (1983), 'Use of classification in online retrieval', *Library Resources and Technical Services*, 27 (1), 76–80.

Vizine-Goetz, Diane (1997a), 'Classification research at OCLC', *Annual Review of OCLC Research 1996*, pp. 27–30. Also available at http://www.purl.org/oclc/review1996

—— (1997b), 'From book classification to knowledge organization: Improving Internet resource description and discovery', *Bulletin of the American Society for Information Science* (October/November), 24–7.

8 UDC in the twenty-first century
I. C. McIlwaine

Introduction

To gaze into the future with a crystal ball is always difficult. Much has happened to the UDC in the last decade of the twentieth century, and it is unlikely that anyone predicting its fate even in 1990 would have foreseen the current situation. Indeed, the publication issued in that year – *The UDC: essays for a new decade* (Gilchrist and Strachan, 1990) – contains a great deal of information that became very out of date well before the turn of the century. The Classification, in particular its management structure, bears little resemblance to the situation thirty years ago when Geoffrey Lloyd wrote his chapter in *Classification in the 1970s* (Lloyd, 1976) though it is depressing to note that some of the revisions that he projects for the near future, such as Photography and Music, are still high on the list of problem classes needing urgent editorial attention. Equally sobering is the fact that many of the proposals that he made for the improvement of the scheme are very similar to those which conclude this present chapter. The UDC remains one of the more widely used of the general systems, especially in those parts of the world where English is not commonly spoken. It cannot, however, in any way rival its parent, the Dewey Decimal Classification, which has itself undergone many radical changes, both in management and in its approach to development in the intervening years. In *Classification in the 1970s*, Lloyd wrote that throughout the first half of the last century the two closely related schemes maintained their parallel structure to such an extent that it was possible for an institution to use them in conjunction with one another, with UDC expanding on the Decimal Classification's broader structure, without any great notational problems. At present, this is no longer the case in many of the main classes of the two schemes, but it is the ambition of the present editors of both to attempt to put the clock back, in this respect at least, and to try to impose a greater correspondence between the structure and notational symbols used in the two systems.

The last decade

Several important events have taken place in the last ten years which will undoubtedly affect the scheme's future revision and development. The first was the foundation, in 1992, of the UDC Consortium (UDCC), when FID together with the publishers of the Dutch, English, French, Japanese and Spanish editions became founder members of the UDCC. The Consortium assumed ownership of UDC on 1 January 1992. One of its first actions was to create an international database which could be the source of many kinds of UDC editions. This is the Master Reference File (MRF), which is currently held at the Royal Library in The Hague, and updated once a year. The text is at present in English only and it is the authoritative version of the Classification. The first published version in hard copy based on this File was that issued by the British Standards Institution in 1993 (BSI, 1993). A new edition has recently been under preparation. For the first six years of its existence Consortium membership has remained the same, but in 1998 VINITI, an organization long connected with the Classification, applied for membership. Conditions of membership of the Consortium require the member to be a publisher in a world language, and membership normally carries with it the exclusive rights to publish in the language of the applicant. It is possible for institutions who do not wish to take on the full obligations of membership of the Consortium to apply for a licence either to publish a version of the Classification in one format (two formats, for example hard copy and CD-ROM, require two licences, and so on) or to mount the Classification on their local networks. This is the preferred route for many publishers issuing editions in languages that are not widely spoken, such as Czech, Polish or Estonian.

In addition to the creation of a machine-readable file, the Consortium has paid particular attention to speeding up procedures for the revision and implementation of new classes of the Classification. With this end in view, the elaborate committee structure described in many textbooks on classification and the slow, democratic processes for revision have been discarded. The Central Classification Committee was dissolved in the 1970s and was replaced by a UDC Management Board which in turn ceased to exist once FID ceased to be the owner of the Classification. In 1993 the Consortium decided to appoint an editor-in-chief and an editorial board with international membership to oversee the content of the UDC and contribute to its revision. Both the editor and the board members are people with full-time commitments elsewhere who act in an advisory capacity. Until 1997 there was a salaried technical director and secretarial assistance. Since the beginning of 1997 the post of technical director has been vacant and instead a research assistant has been employed to assist the editor with work on revision. Revisions, other than those undertaken by the research assistant herself, are commissioned. All revisions are quality checked by an authority in the field, normally an institution specializing in the subject concerned, and usually one that uses the scheme in practice. *Extensions and corrections to the UDC* has also altered in format from 1993 onwards. It continues to appear annually, but in addition to publishing approved revisions, it also includes proposals on which comment is invited, reports from users, articles on the Classification and a bibliography of recent publications. The Office and Secretariat of the UDC Consortium remain in The Hague where the Master Reference File is located.

One of the major advantages of the new situation is the conversion of the Classification into a machine-readable format. This has had largely but not entirely beneficial results. It is now in a manageable form, it can be revised much more easily than before, and it is searchable on terms that appear in the text or as examples, giving much greater scope for diverse approaches than the normal indexes to the printed versions of the scheme. It is a 'standard' version, and this means that the edition known for 98 years as the full edition, consisting of over 220 000 direct divisions, no longer exists. There is now one master version, and it consists of just over 61 000 entries. This roughly approximates to what used to be known as a 'medium' edition. The UDCC does not authorize any numbers that do not occur in the Master Reference File, though individual publishers may, if they so wish, extend the basic text into greater detail, provided that they make it clear that any expansion that they create is not authorized. Normally this actually means that some publishers continue to issue extended tables (similar in size to the old full edition), but no work has been done on revising them beyond medium level under the auspices of the UDCC. This can justifiably be seen as one of the shortcomings of the new regime, but currently there are no resources to maintain the scheme at a more detailed level. It is also the intention to make sure that the development of the Classification is even throughout, and at present this is not the case, even in the standard text. It would be much more difficult to impose such a policy if the 'full' tables were to become the standard text. At the beginning of the 1990s there was in existence a medium edition in English (BSI, 1985–88) which was in machine-readable format, and this greatly eased the task of creating the Master Reference File as it could be used as the basis on which to build the standard version. There are only small sections of the old full edition in machine-readable format, so the task of creating such a large database would have been and remains beyond the capability of the limited finances on which the UDC has to survive. In addition to what will in future become known as the Standard Edition (that is the old Medium Edition), many versions are published in smaller sizes, such as the Pocket Edition which is the latest of the British Standards Institution's products in their range of English editions (BSI, 1998).

To assist users of the UDC, FID published a *Guide to the Use of the UDC* (McIlwaine, 1995) in English in 1993, and a revised edition two years later. This has been translated into Japanese, French, Spanish and Czech, and a Portuguese translation is in preparation. It in no way supersedes previous guides, particularly the one produced by Jack Mills for the British Standards Institution in 1963 (*Guide to the Universal Decimal Classification*), but it provides help in the actual application of the scheme in a practical situation and includes many examples of class numbers. In addition to assisting in the creation of classmarks, it contains a chapter on the use of the Classification in an online environment.

Present situation

One of the problems with the UDC is that, unlike the other major general classification schemes, it is not aiming at a known and predictable market (for a brief outline of its history and recent developments see McIlwaine, 1997a). Both the Dewey Decimal Classification and the Library of Congress Classification are designed for and used in well-documented and defined environments. The UDC, on the other hand, may be used for the classification of a highly technical and specialized institution, such as the Institute of Electrical Engineers in the United Kingdom, and for a range of public library systems, for example in Spain. Additionally, it is used in many university libraries, especially in those areas of Eastern Europe where funding is scant, and languages other than English are spoken. Although the Dewey Decimal Classification is forging ahead with translations into languages such as Russian and Chinese, it has yet to tackle those languages such as Croatian, Estonian, Romanian or even Japanese (Nippon DC being a different scheme), where the UDC has for many years been the standard. The Classification therefore has to be capable of application across a wide range of different situations; it is also applied in situations where, although computerization is now the norm, there are few resources to implement changes; hence radical revisions are frequently unpopular. One of the greatest problems, therefore, is to maintain the scheme in a form that satisfies its current and faithful users, and yet to make it sufficiently dynamic and receptive to new environments so that it can attract new users and encourage its application in contexts other than those for which it has traditionally been employed. Its use, for example, for the organization of the Royal Collection in the United Kingdom, where artefacts of every kind as well as books are classified by it, demonstrates its features to advantage in a way that has not always been capitalized upon in the past.

At present, however, the editorial and management procedures and structures are much better organized and coherent, and the financial situation, while far from ideal, is much more favourable than has been the case for the past twenty years. This is largely because the procedures are now in the hands of a few people in regular communication with one another. It must be stressed, though, that this situation is totally against all the fundamental principles that have prevailed for its organization throughout most of the last century. The Classification cannot in any way compete with its fellow general schemes in terms of the infrastructure and financial backing, nor in terms of the availability of classmarks on records distributed by cooperatives such as OCLC. In particular, it lacks a link to a large library where it is in daily use, providing a source of literary warrant and a testing ground for revisions as well as the expertise of a team of classifiers applying it in a practical situation. This is in part desirable since, unlike DDC and LCC, it has always had a wider remit and is adaptable to a greater range of different situations, both bibliographical and other. The new English Pocket Edition, for example, is being marketed as suitable for the organization of personal computer files, amongst other uses.

Revision programme

As noted above, major changes in the Classification introduced too frequently are unpopular with existing users, but the Classification as it stands at present is in need of much attention. There are several classes that need completely restructuring and there is a programme in place to accomplish this gradually over the next ten years. A new table for Computer Science and Technology was published in 1996, relocating it in 004 (it is in the same position in the Dewey Decimal Classification). Work has been in progress on totally new classifications for Physics and Medicine (the latter described later) which were due to be completed in 1999. Classes that have been in the process of gradual revision include Chemistry, Mathematics, Religion and Astronomy. Cinema and Photography have also been reviewed and new tables were due to be produced in 1998 or 1999. High on the list of priorities for attention were Nuclear Science and Technology (which should have been partially improved when the new Physics classification was completed), Electronics, Education, Architecture and Building. But the millennium dawned before all these reached completion.

Hand in hand with this major overhaul is the general tidying up of the

Classification. As the tables are at present, there is a series of Auxiliary Tables and the Main Tables. Strictly speaking, the Main Tables should contain no compound concepts, since all should be able to be expressed through the use of the auxiliaries (which include the use of the colon, to join any one piece of the Classification to another). This is far from being the present state of affairs. Throughout the Classification there are many terms listed in combination with others which should be expressed as two separate concepts, and even in the Auxiliary Tables the same concepts may be repeated in more than one place with different notations. One example of this was Table 1i – Common auxiliaries of points of view (Robinson, 1997). This table contained a mixture of concepts, some of which could be easily expressed through the use of the colon, some of which belonged to either Table 1d – Common auxiliaries of form – or Table 1k-05 – Common auxiliaries of persons, – and others which were 'Property' terms, rather than points of view. This table of points of view has now been cancelled, and the various parts of it redistributed to their logical places; a new table of common properties was developed for implementation in 1998. This is part of a long-term plan (yet another of the future ambitions referred to in Lloyd's chapter – Lloyd, 1976) to equip the Classification with a series of common subdivisions to cover generally recurring concepts introduced by the hyphen, and dispense with many of the special auxiliaries that occur throughout individual classes and can easily be overlooked by an unwary user or one unaccustomed to the printed format, which differs according to the house style of the various publishers. At the same time, Table 1k-05 – Common auxiliaries of persons, is being overhauled, and all references to persons in compounded concepts in the main classes are being taken out. This is in order to create a much simpler classification, in the long term, so that concepts can easily be retrieved, especially in an automated system, rather than being buried in compounded notation which cannot be detected by computer because they are not clearly distinguished in their notation. The intention is to tidy the auxiliaries first, while checking the tables to remove anomalies, and then to concentrate more determinedly on disciplines that are not very urgent. Part of the same plan is to cease the use of parallel division whereby one part of the Classification is divided like another. Class 9 was the first to be unravelled, and areas are no longer part of the main numbers at 91 and 93/99, in Geography and History, but are simply appended to the root numbers 91 and 94 respectively, enclosed in brackets in the normal way. Dates, in History, are similarly expressed through the use of Table 1g – Common auxiliaries of time (BSI, 1997). So, the History of the United Kingdom now appears thus:

94(420)	History of England and Great Britain *Class here the history of the United Kingdom as a whole. For the history of the countries of the UK individually see 94(411), 94(415) and 94(429)...*
94(420) "-/1066"	Prehistory, Roman and Anglo-Saxon period
94(420) "1066/1154"	Norman kings, 1066–1154
94(420) "1154/1399"	House of Plantagenet, 1154–1399
...	
94(420) "1910/1936"	George V, 1910–1936
94(420) "1936"	Edward VIII, 1936
94(420) "1936/1952"	George VI, 1936–1952
94(420) "1952/..."	Elizabeth II, 1952–

At the same time, the opportunity was taken to remove the history of the two world wars from its previous location under the History of Europe to the more logical position of World History:

94(100) "1914/1918"	First World War, 1914–1918
94(100) "1939/1945"	Second World War, 1939–1945

Medicine: a special case

There are, however, some disciplines that are in very urgent need of attention. Medicine is a case in point. This was given careful consideration in 1993 when users were consulted about the revision procedures. At that time, serious consideration was given to leaving the classification for Medicine as it was, since the majority of medical libraries all over the world had switched their allegiance, in the interests of standardization and conformity with MeSH, to the National Library of Medicine Classification. This proposal was met with dismay from the many general or scientific libraries that use the UDC and have sizeable collections of medical works, without being exclusively devoted to Medicine. It was therefore decided to revise Medicine thoroughly and, as the result of work undertaken by Professor Williamson at the University of Toronto investigating the feasibility of turning the revised Bliss Bibliographic Classification tables into a UDC-like notation (Williamson, 1992), an agreement was entered into with the Bliss Classification Association for an exchange of tables under certain conditions. The first trials were carried out in 1993–94 (Williamson and McIlwaine, 1993) and reports on progress have been provided annually in *Extensions and Corrections to the UDC*. The project was completed by 1999 and represents a completely new classification for Medicine in UDC, with a changed citation order focused on the Persons (for example Gynaeocology and Obstetrics,

Paediatrics, and so on) then the System, which results in 'actions' such as surgery or pathology being subordinated to the appropriate part of the body, unless the item being classified is concerned with the action in general.

Cooperation with other schemes

The pooling of expertise and interchange of information with editors of other classification schemes is not limited to the agreement with the Bliss Classification Association (McIlwaine, 1997b). In days when resources are scarce it makes sense for editors to keep in contact with one another. A recent feature at the annual IFLA conference has been a report from each of the editors of general schemes who are present on activities and developments at the meeting of the Section on Bibliographic Control. This provides an opportunity for users to keep in touch with developments and to make contact if they wish. The editors of DDC and UDC meet regularly and exchange information on revisions. Negotiations are under way for the publication of a joint area table. This will use the same notation for both schemes, but will include alternatives for Eastern Europe, which is the section of the area subdivisions where there is the greatest diversity between the two classifications, and which will have the greatest impact on UDC users if UDC notations are abandoned in favour of DDC ones. This is the beginning of the greater harmonization between the two classifications referred to in the opening paragraph and has certainly proved the way forward into this century. One of the UDC's greatest advantages is that its base remains reasonably close to that of DDC, but it has a range of additional features that provide the facility for the expression of concepts in far greater depth than is possible with the parent classification. The UDC can complement the Dewey Decimal Classification by providing greater detail and by using clearly distinguishable facet indicators which, although they create problems for shelving and other routine library practices, are not a difficulty for the retrieval of information in a machine-oriented world. To use the Dewey Decimal Classification as a basis and expand it using UDC when greater detail or more flexibility is needed, while leaving existing users of either classification to continue their present practices, would be a sensible way forward. The revision of a class as a joint project is one of the plans that the editors would like to see initiated, as a pilot and without obligation on either scheme to implement the result, so as to find out whether there is a future in such cooperation.

Future potential

At present the UDC is in a better position to move forward than it has been for some years. Its publishers are now issuing the Classification in a range of formats, including CD-ROM. There are proposals for bilingual CD-ROMs, and agreements are being worked out between the British Standards Institution and the respective other-language publishers to implement these. The next step is to make the Master Reference File a multilingual product. This sounds more straightforward than it is because although what in the past would have been referred to as Medium Editions exist in several languages, all were produced at different times, and therefore do not conform to the Master Reference File in its current state, quite apart from the linguistic problems that would need considerable editorial attention. Also, it is usual for individual-language publishers to include detail that is appropriate for that particular language edition so, for example, the French Medium Edition will have the examples in class 9 spelt out for matter of interest to the French-speaking world, rather than the detailed set of examples drawing on British history to be found in the English-language text. A multilingual database, however, is one of the proposals being given very serious attention. If it comes into being it will provide a very powerful retrieval tool as it will have the facility to act as a switching language, and use the UDC notation as a means of finding information across languages, without the user being aware of what is happening.

Nowadays, most research into retrieval tools is based on the use of natural language. This results in obvious problems if the searcher can be satisfied by information in more than one language. People clearly prefer to search using natural language, but if a classification can act as a control and provide a structure that is not evident to the user, that considerably enhances the retrieval potentiality of a system. The UDC possesses that intrinsic potential, both in the hierarchical structure of its notation and through the range of auxiliary devices provided for linking related concepts. The revision of the scheme that is at present under way, devoted to unravelling the compounded concepts rather than creating a range of totally new classes, will also improve the structure of the Classification. Above all, it will make it much more amenable to use in searching very large databases, not least the Internet, in a more structured manner than is possible at present through the use of the various search engines that are currently available. Many of these rely solely on the use of words, and frequently any form of categorization that they embody is full of cross-classifications, especially through the mixture of subject and form approaches, embodied in such labels as 'Reference', 'Libraries', 'History', 'Travel', and so on. The notation of the UDC, which historically has always been held up as a problem, causes far fewer difficulties in an automated environment than it does in a manual one. Once the compounds have been eliminated, the notation will enable the searcher to identify positively each term used in the Classification, and the context in which it occurs. The elimination of compounds and of parallel division, whereby one part of the Classification is divided like another, as used to be done in the Dewey Decimal Classification when the instruction 'Divide like' was used, will clarify the meaning of each concept uniquely.

The closing of the gap in general structure between DDC and UDC by such devices as the use of common tables for certain recurring topics, such as areas, will pave the way for future collaboration and improved standardization. The possibility of extending this practice to the creation of one or two compatible main classes, extended further through the use of the various synthetic devices that UDC possesses but Dewey lacks, offers a fruitful way forward this century. Obviously, classes need revision, and this has to be done at two levels: the continual patching up and correcting of errors or incorporation of new concepts on the one hand, and the total overhaul of long outdated or unusable classes such as Physics or Music on the other. The vacancy of class 4 is something that troubles some users. At present, there are no firm plans for filling it. One possibility would be to use it as a 'parking' device into which newly revised classes could be placed, leaving the originals in place for those who did not wish to avail themselves of the revision. The order of main classes does not conform to any real logic for the twenty-first century, so this could be done, but it is intellectually unsatisfying to create further breaks in a familiar sequence. Clearly, there are powerful attractions in extending the science classes back, as was the original proposal, and having a greater range of notations available. The possibility of putting disciplines like Psychology and Environmental Studies into class 4 have not been overlooked. If a new class for Psychology were created, and it is a subject that sorely needs revision, there is plenty of space already in class 1 for it, with blocks of unused numbers and no extensive subdivision for any other section of that class. A preferable option would be to relocate the Biological sciences, Psychology and Medicine and put them all together, possibly with Agriculture, into class 4. Class 62 could then be extended in both directions to cover 61/63.

Wholesale relocations on this scale tend to be unpopular with existing users though they might be attractive to other potential ones. One major drawback at present is that UDC classmarks rarely appear on any records generated by cooperatives. This is not a situation that shows any sign of changing, but there are now certain organizations, such as the British Standards Institution, which give advice on the application of the Classification. If a market for the use of such expertise on a wider basis were seen to be economic, services such as this could be extended and turned into an agency supplying preclassified information. The principal reason for the lack of such information at present is that the UDC is not based in a single library such as the Library of Congress, unlike the other widely used general schemes. If it were, it could no longer claim to be 'Universal' but the situation does create certain drawbacks.

The death of UDC has been foretold for the past forty years. It not only lives on, but it now has its own Web page (http://zeus.slais.ucl.ac.uk/udc/udc.htm) and other benefits of late twentieth-century electronic communication. If it can capitalize on its strengths, manage to update itself without upsetting all its users in the process, and find suitable applications to extend its use, it has great potential as a retrieval tool that will last well into this, the third century of its existence.

References

BSI (British Standards Institution) (1963), *Guide to the Universal Decimal Classification* (BS 1000C: 1963), London: BSI.

────── (1985–88), Universal Decimal Classification, *International Medium Edition. English text.* (BS 1000M: 1985–88) (FID Publication no. 571), London: BSI, 2 vols.

────── (1993), Universal Decimal Classification, *International Medium Edition, English text. Edition 2.* (BS 1000M: 1993). London: BSI, 2 vols.

────── (1997), Universal Decimal Classification, *International Medium Edition, English text. Edition 2. Supplement no. 3.* (BS 1000M: Supplement no. 3: 1997), London: BSI.

────── (1998), Universal Decimal Classification, *Pocket English Edition* (BS 1000P), London: BSI.

Gilchrist, A. and Strachan, D. (eds) (1990), *The UDC: essays for a new decade*, London: Aslib.

Lloyd, G. A. (1976), 'Universal Decimal Classification', In A. Maltby (ed.), *Classification in the 1970s*, revised edn, London: Bingley, pp. 99–118.

McIlwaine, I. C. (1995), *Guide to the Use of the UDC*, revised edn (FID 703), The Hague: International Federation for Information and Documentation.

McIlwaine, I. C. (1997a), 'The Universal Decimal Classification: some factors concerning its origins, development and influence', *Journal of the American Society of Information Scientists*, **48** (4), 331–9.

McIlwaine, I. C. (1997b), 'Classification schemes: consultation with users and co-operation between editors', *Cataloging and Classification Quarterly*, **24** (1/2), 81–95. Also published in J. R. Shearer and A. R. Thomas (eds) (1997), *Cataloging and Classification: trends, transformations, teaching and training*, New York and London: Haworth Press, pp. 81–95.

Robinson, G. (1997), 'An odd point of view: some reflections on Table 1i in the UDC common auxiliaries', *Extensions and Corrections to the UDC*, **19**, 29–31.

Williamson, N. J. (1992), 'Restructuring UDC: problems and possibilities', in N. J. Williamson and M. Hudon (eds), *Classification Research for Knowledge Representation and Organization: proceedings of the 5th International Study Conference on Classification Research, Toronto, Canada, June 24th–28th 1991* (FID 698), Amsterdam and London: Elsevier.

Williamson, N. J. and McIlwaine, I. C. (1993), 'Future revisions of UDC: report on a feasibility study for restructuring', *Extensions and Corrections to the UDC*, **16**, 11–17.

9 The Library of Congress Classification
Lois Mai Chan and Theodora L. Hodges

Introduction

The second millennium for those who follow the Gregorian calendar, and the century mark for the Library of Congress Classification (LCC), occurred at almost the same time. (The decision to develop a new classification for the Library of Congress was made in 1900, and a provisional outline was drawn up in 1901 (LaMontagne, 1961).) It is particularly fitting, therefore, that the current vitality of the LCC system – and its likely prospects – be evaluated at this time.

Recent developments

The 1990s have been a rich time for the Library of Congress Classification. Among LCC milestones for the decade are

- the Library of Congress's decision, in 1998, to replace its automated system – in use since the 1960s – with the integrated system Voyager;
- the completion of the project – begun in 1993 – to convert full schedule data into machine-readable form under the USMARC Classification Format;
- the creation of the tool Classification Plus, a quarterly CD-ROM-based product that will eventually include the full text of LCC plus all of Library of Congress Subject Headings, with links between the two where appropriate;
- a considerable acceleration in the rate of issuing revised schedules;
- many modifications to tables and indexes, to resolve inconsistencies shown up by the conversion;

- the completion of several new schedules, particularly subclasses KL–KWX and KZ in Class K Law, subclass JZ in Class J Political Science, and subclass ZA in Class Z Bibliography and Library Science; and
- the use of LCC classification data in online browsers and search guides and directories for organizing and navigating Internet resources.

These developments are discussed in detail below.

The integrated system Voyager

The Library of Congress announced its plans to implement Voyager, a new integrated system from the Endeavor Information Systems, in 1999. It is not yet certain what operations will be the first to be brought under that system. Conversion will undoubtedly be a monumental undertaking. While it is too early to predict what impact the new system will have on LCC specifically, it is safe to assume that it will affect all aspects of bibliographic control at the Library of Congress, including its classification scheme. Furthermore, anyone who has been involved with implementing a new computer system – or even read accounts of such an undertaking – will realize that great upheavals are in store.

Conversion of LCC to machine-readable form

For several reasons, the conversion of its schedules to machine-readable form – which was done using the USMARC Classification Format (1991) – was an especially important development for LCC. For one thing, it enabled much more efficient production of the print schedules. For another, it made it possible to develop and issue Classification Plus. And for a third, it has greatly facilitated revision, not only of whole schedules but also of tables and indexes.

The conversion project was a long one. Its inception was in the late 1980s, when, recognizing the need for a MARC format for communicating and storing classification data, the Library of Congress began the development of the USMARC Classification Format in consultation with the editorial staff and advisory committee of the Dewey Decimal Classification. With the completion and publication of the Format in 1991, the Library embarked on the ambitious project of converting the LCC schedules to machine-readable form. Work began in 1993 with Class H, and was carried out with the assistance of outside contractors as well as by the Library's own staff. Conversion was completed in 1996. An important thing to realize, in connection with this project, is that very little modification or revision was done during the conversion process.

Classification Plus

Machine-readable LCC records are directly available to staff at LC through the Minaret software package. As a service to users outside of LC, the Library has incorporated its machine-readable classification data into Classification Plus (1996 and 1995), which is a full-text, Windows-based CD-ROM tool that is produced with the Folio software. Classification Plus, which is updated quarterly, also includes the full text of Library of Congress Subject Headings, with links between LCSH and LCC where appropriate.

Classification Plus is a very useful tool for cataloguing agencies and others who use the LCC system, not only for its links between LCC captions and LCSH headings but for its sophisticated access provisions. It allows searching by keywords, using Boolean logic, wildcard characters, proximity specification, and truncation; furthermore, several files can be displayed at once, so a user can compare data from different class schedules. It also allows browsing class numbers up and down the hierarchy.

New editions of schedules

With the schedules in machine-readable form, the Library is now able to produce print schedules directly from records in the USMARC Classification Format. This capability greatly facilitates the revision and updating of individual schedules and indexes, so that new editions are now being produced at much closer intervals. Since the beginning of the conversion project, the following schedules have been reworked and new editions have been issued, some of them twice: B–BJ Philosophy, Psychology; C Auxiliary science of history, DS–DX Asia, Africa, Oceania, Gypsies; E–F History: America; H Social sciences (1994, 1997); J Political Science (1997, 1998); KD Law of the United Kingdom and Ireland; KZ Law of Nations (1997, 1998); L Education; N Fine arts; P–PA Philology and general linguistics, Classical languages and literature; PQ Romance literatures; P–PZ Tables; Q Science; R Medicine; S Agriculture; T Technology; U–V Military and Naval sciences; and Z Bibliography and Library science. Most of these have been cumulations of the original schedules with additions and changes since the last edition.

However, as time and personnel permit, more fundamental, intellectual revision is undertaken. To maintain stability, thorough revision is often performed on selected subclasses. Among other recent efforts is the systematic revision of subclasses H through HG, where greater consistency among subclasses has been achieved; subclasses affected include those covering statistics, economic theory and history, management, labour and personnel management, finance, and the other core business subjects. According to a recent report,

> In this activity, guidelines are being applied to achieve improvements as follows: (1) form and chronological sub-arrangements are being standardized; (2) geographic lists are being expanded and updated; (3) topical captions are being revised to reflect LCSH terminology with notes added to clarify usage; (4) unnecessarily complex sub-arrangements are being simplified while overlapping or difficult to distinguish topics are being consolidated; and (5) legal topics within this class are being referred to class K (Law). (Library of Congress, Bibliographic Enrichment Advisory Team, 1997)

Subclasses in K have also been reworked, with increased consistency as a goal.

One of the ways to achieve uniformity in the major divisions in a class has been to establish models for arranging subclasses and divisions. Models for development have been a feature of LCC since Charles Martel posited his seven points for subdivision within a class, subclass, or subject. With the renewed focus on consistency, the need for patterns or models for topical division has received more attention, and some have been developed recently. One example is the general pattern of arrangement of divisions under each country in the schedules for Class D:

1) General works
2) Description and travel
3) Antiquities. Social life and customs, etc.
4) History
5) Local history and description

Because it is concerned about the upheaval attendant on major reclassification, the Library of Congress is reluctant to make large adjustments in previously developed classes to bring them into full conformity with these patterns. Nevertheless, the application of the models in new developments ensures a degree of consistency among subject areas being developed for the first time.

New subclasses

The decade of the 1990s saw considerable activity in the development of new subclasses. Of particular interest to information retrieval is the new subclass ZA, Information Resources, completed and implemented in 1996. It is Class K Law that is especially worthy of note, however, because work on that class has taken longer than that on any other class in LCC. It was not until 1969 that the first schedule in Class K, Subclass KF Law of the United States, was published in a preliminary edition. Since then, other K schedules appeared as they were completed; by 1990, however, no schedules covering the law of areas outside of the Americas and Europe had been published. Thus, the appearance of the schedule KL–KWX Law of Asia and Eurasia, Africa, Pacific Area, and Antarctica, marked a milestone when it was published in two volumes in 1993. Another new K schedule is Subclass KZ Law of Nations, which was published in 1997; KZ was developed in conjunction with Subclass JZ, Political Science–International Relations, and the two together supersede Subclass JX International Relations. With the publication of Subclass KZ, the development of Class K with respect to comparative and uniform private and public international law on the global and regional level as well as domestic law on the jurisdictional level is complete. The remaining subclasses to be developed are KB–KBZ for theocratic legal systems.

Modifications to tables and indexes

Tables

As noted earlier, conversion of the schedules to conform to the MARC Classification Format was relatively mechanical; little modification or revision was carried out during conversion. Not surprisingly, several facts became glaringly evident when the data from separate schedules were merged into one database. Foremost among these is inconsistency, both in table application and in the indexes. Rebecca S. Guenther summarizes the problems in the following statement:

> As different schedules were converted, it became obvious that the application of tables was highly inconsistent throughout the scheme. In some cases tables appeared at the end of the schedule, in others within the text, in others by footnotes referencing other locations. Even more disturbing was the fact that how those tables are applied to a number was inconsistent. In some cases the number from the table is appended to the base number; in other cases it is necessary to perform addition to calculate a number resulting from adding from a table to a base number ... (Guenther, 1996)

Thus, while the automated system enabled many welcome improvements in the appearance and layout of the printed schedules, it also highlighted the desirability of certain changes in their format, particularly in the display of internal and auxiliary tables. As a result, both in print and CD-ROM versions, many internal tables which were previously scattered throughout each schedule have been grouped together and renumbered. In the print version of a schedule, many of them have been moved to the end, just before the index.

Other efforts toward uniformity in respect to LCC tables include increasing the use of free-floating tables, reformatting the tables within individual classes, and trying to harmonize similar tables in separate schedules within specific classes. It should be remembered in this respect that, unlike tables in many other classification schemes, most tables in LCC are unique to individual classes, sometimes even to subclasses. It has long been recognized that this disparity makes the application of the system difficult, particularly for beginners, and it is not only since the system's conversion to machine-readable form that efforts have been made toward alleviation. For example, in 1982 tables for authors and individual works used throughout Class P were consolidated and published in a separate volume. Likewise, a full review of Class K form division tables was undertaken: many tables were condensed, and redundant entries were eliminated. As a result, a set of generic form division tables was designed, which are to be applied uniformly in all Class K schedules except the common law schedules of KF, KD, and KE.

Indexes

Rebecca Guenther's analysis, extracted above, also referred to indexes:

> The indexes to the schedules provide rich terminology, but they vary greatly because schedules were developed individually and revised at different times. The depth of indexing from one schedule to the next is dependent upon the subject matter and the perspective of the indexer. As the different schedules are being brought together into one master classification database these inconsistencies have become obvious. (Guenther, 1996, footnote 4)

Although revising indexes is never a trivial task, it is nevertheless one that is greatly facilitated once entries can be manipulated by machine. In part for this reason, many individual schedule indexes have been extensively re-examined and revamped in recent years. In respect to a general index to the whole Classification, however, the picture is less rosy. The existence of the electronic system makes it almost a trivial matter to compile a merged index to all the schedules, and this has been done on a trial basis. However, such mergers of individual indexes have revealed incompatibilities in vocabulary and inconsistencies in style and depth; the former, having to do with terminology, are particularly glaring and unacceptable. Such variations are not surprising given that the schedules were developed almost independently of each other and have largely been maintained independently ever since. In any term list, but especially so in a list compiled from disparate sources, reconciling incompatibilities requires long and intensive intellectual input. The Library of Congress recognizes this fact, and also realizes that the first stage of developing a merged index must be to draft indexing guidelines. At the present time, the need for resources for such a project must compete against many other demands on the system. It would therefore be unrealistic to expect a high-quality general index to the whole classification in the near future.

Use of LCC in organizing Internet resources

Increasingly, local online systems and search engines are using hierarchical or classification-based browsers to organize and navigate Internet resources. This is a logical development; after all, classification was devised in the beginning as a response to the need for organizing large amounts of knowledge and information. To those in librarianship and information retrieval, it comes as a validation of their expertise that with the exponential growth of resources available on the Internet, the value of using hierarchical or classification structures to facilitate access to Web resources has begun to be recognized and appreciated. It may be that the reason for such recognition is that classification frameworks can be used in two ways: to provide browsing capability and to facilitate navigating. Among the advantages of using classification-based browsers are improved subject browsing, the capacity to broaden and narrow searches, the availability of context for search terms, the ability to partition and manipulate large databases, and the potential facilitation of multilingual access and improved interaction with other services (Chan, 1995).

Gerry McKiernan has been monitoring World Wide Web browsers that are based on existing classification schemes (McKiernan, n.d.). For example, among the sites he had identified as of late 1998, five sites had installed subject organization devices (also called subject guides or subject trees) that are based on LCC. However, among those that purport to be based on a particular existing scheme, there are large variations in the categories used and in the depth – available levels – of searching. Very few sites allow searchers to penetrate very far into hierarchical subject displays.

Two of the more promising projects that are using LCC as a means of organizing Internet resources are:

CyberStacks at http://www.public.iastate.edu/~CYBERSTACKS/ and The Scout Report Signpost at http:/www.signpost.org/signpost/index.html

Downloaded Web pages from these two systems appear as an appendix to this chapter.

CyberStacks (McKiernan, 1997a) was created by Gerry McKiernan, who recalls the reasons for choosing LCC to organize it:

> The Library of Congress Classification is a well-established scheme that has been used for generations by libraries worldwide for organizing a variety of publications and media. Within its schedules, this classification system not only denotes subject coverage and content, but information format and conceptual relationships as well. It is believed that a classification system with the features found within the Library of Congress scheme offers appropriate context and structure that can facilitate identification of relevant WWW and other Internet resources. (McKiernan, 1997b)

Scout Report Signpost is an Internet resource discovery service provided by the Internet Scout Project to 'guide the U.S. higher education community to quality electronic resources' (Glassel and Wells, 1997). The resources selected and described are divided into broad disciplinary areas by relevant main and subclasses in LCC. Summarizing the development of Signpost, Glassel and Wells describe how LCC is used in that system:

> Disciplines are assigned one- to three-lettered class codes . . . to form a hierarchical tree or classification system. . . . Each subdivision contains a hypertext link to a list of the resources assigned to the respective class code.
> Signpost contains . . . modifications to the LC classification system. [Class letters are used without class number extensions; many items are assigned two different class codes; and explanatory notes are provided to selected LCC class and/or subclass descriptions.] (Glassel and Wells, 1997, note 10, pp. 38–40)

The same article goes on to give the reason for choosing the LC classification for Signpost: 'Since the Internet Scout Project assists the U.S. higher education and research community, this taxonomy was chosen because it presumably requires little to no learning curve to be used by its intended audience' (Glassel and Wells, 1997, note 10, p. 40).

Conclusions

Arriving in the new millennium

What can be said about the current state of the Library of Congress classification system? How well is it adapting to the demands now made upon it, demands that are considerably different from those that prompted its initial development?

All signs are that it is faring well, given its age and the general recognition that it lacks an overall coherent and logical structure from a theoretical point of view. New schedules, and revised editions of older ones, are being issued at a rate that was unthinkable before the schedules were converted to the MARC format. Minor changes are also being made at a commendable rate: captions and schedule placements that reflect usage of prior times are being updated or removed, the system's many tables are being made more uniform, and individual schedule indexes are being re-examined and revamped. The system's conversion into machine-readable form, it seems, was a fountain of youth for LCC because of automation's potential for increased productivity. What matters in judging the current health of the system is that the LC staff has not squandered this potential but has made good use of it.

Another sign of well-being is the system's apparent continued popularity. After a century of use by libraries, the Library of Congress Classification remains an eminently practical system. Over the years, many libraries have adopted the system for their own use, probably in part for its substance and in part for its usefulness as a technical services aid. Nor have adoptions been limited to the United States; many foreign libraries have apparently found LCC an effective classification tool, even with needed adaptations to fit local literary warrant, and, it can be conjectured, have found it a help in technical services matters as well. Not to be ignored in this connection is that LCC and other Library of Congress products are dependable and are judged to be of high quality. Supported as the Library is by a major government, in a relatively stable political and economic environment, its classification schedules are continuously revised, and the classification placements assigned by LC subject cataloguers are generally considered satisfactory. All the above factors indicate the system's strength.

On the question of adaptability there are positive signs as well. One measure of adaptability is that the Library has continued, and even expanded, activities that reflect its sense of responsibility to the profession as a whole and to the outside institutions that have adopted its system. In the beginning, LCC was conceived and developed as an internal tool for the Library's collection; its architects had not thought that it would be used in a wider sphere (Martel, 1929). But the system did prove relatively popular with other libraries – particularly those with very large collections – almost from the time it was first presented to the library community, and all along the Library has been responsive to the fact that such institutions need quick access to current information on changes in the system. The most recent case in point, in this respect, is the development of Classification Plus. Earlier examples include the various ways in which LC cataloguing records have been made available to others: printed cards, electronically through networks, and, more recently, on the Internet through LOCIS (Library of Congress Information System). Another example is the publication and maintenance of the two subject cataloguing manuals, one on classification and the other on shelflisting (Library of Congress, Office for Subject Cataloging Policy, 1995).

In the same sphere – responsibility to the profession and to participating libraries – what the Library has *not* done is also of interest. It is not only theorists of classification who realize that the world map of knowledge changes shape continually, sometimes gradually, sometimes in paradigm leaps, and that a classification scheme is more effective the more it reflects such changes. Classificationists are also painfully aware of this. Those responsible for a given area in a classification scheme must dream about being able to make the schedules for that area conform more closely to current notions of how topics within it are either interrelated or related to other areas previously thought to be outside the area's bounds. But for many established areas, hundreds of thousands of texts that may still be of potential interest have been arranged on shelves under extant schedules, and no matter how superior a thoroughly revised scheme may be, it is not much help to users if all potentially useful material is not reclassified under it. And large-scale reclassification is not an option for many libraries. Mindful of the burden that major schedule changes place on participating libraries, the Library has gone slow on deep-seated revision, confining its revision efforts to those relatively small parts of the schedules that are furthest out of synchronicity with the currently accepted state of a field. (The Library has garnered some criticism on this score, criticism that is in some ways warranted, but the same caution can also be seen as a sign of the moral health of the institution.)

Another piece of evidence regarding adaptability is the creation of the new Bibliography and Library Science subclass ZA Information Resources. For this burgeoning field, material had been scattered in various areas of the Classification; in Subclass ZA it was finally gathered together in a logical and potentially very useful array. In K Law, the publication of KZ Law of Nations, developed as it was in conjunction with JX Political Science–International Relations, with the two together superseding JX International Relations, is also a sign of adapting to current conditions. (Other new developments in the K schedules, commendable as they are, are a case of going forward with an ongoing task.)

A third encouraging piece in the adaptability picture is the Library's decision to replace its very old automated system with a new one. All agencies handling large amounts of data know what an albatross a relatively primitive automation protocol can be, yet reluctance to move to a better system is very strong because of budgetary and personnel constraints as well as the disruption that often accompanies such a change. The Library of Congress has overcome the obstacles and is now in a position to move forward.

Readiness to adapt to new situations, and willingness to maintain a scheme in such a way that it can afford hospitality to all aspects of a changed information scene, are not all that it takes to be able to do so. Matters of available resources aside, there are substantive roadblocks. Traditional classification systems were designed to accommodate traditional publications, in an environment in which what is to be classed arrives in more-or-less internally cohesive 'chunks' which usually carry with them some indication of how they mesh with what has gone before. When there are few such indications, and a body of orphan literature treating similar matters builds up, classifiers realize that the scheme they work with needs adjustment if the new material is to be adequately accommodated. The key to such adjustment is exposure to newly published material – most of which, in the book world, comes automatically to the Library of Congress through copyright regulations. Comparative exposure to all that is posted on the Internet is beyond the Library's reach – indeed, beyond the reach of any single agency one can contemplate. It seems unlikely, therefore, that LCC can ever be a vehicle for more than broad bibliographical control over Internet postings.

Next steps

It seems, judging from the recent past, that despite its limitations the Library of Congress Classification will begin the twenty-first century with prospects of a viable future before it. It has shown recent evidence of renewed vitality, with no indication that its rate of improvement will slow noticeably unless its move to a new automated system absorbs all its efforts for an appreciable length of time. Whether in the long run it can be a significant player in online retrieval, for the Internet as well as in more traditional vehicles, depends in part on whether those responsible for the system see such a role as one of its functions.

A coherent plan for the future that would be made available to the information community, not just for information but for feedback, can be a means towards ensuring a productive future for the LCC. The Library of Congress has taken initial steps towards improving the Classification. Since 1995, the Cataloging Policy and Support Office, in consultation with Lois Mai Chan, has begun a deliberation on the future directions of LCC in general and an analysis of the merged index in particular. The observations and recommendations are relevant here. They are very briefly summarized below.

Assumptions underlying the analysis

1 Shelving and browsing functions place different demands on a classification. For the former, maintaining a high degree of stability is an

important requirement. For the latter, logical arrangement assumes priority. However, while LCC has the potential of becoming a useful online retrieval tool, for most users – at least for now – the main function of LCC is shelf-arrangement. Indeed, for many libraries, easy access to shelf numbers is one of the most important reasons for adopting LCC. Moreover, there is at present little evidence of a strong demand from LCC users, either within the Library of Congress or outside, for drastic changes in the system's overall structure.

2 Eventually, most users – cataloguers as well as those using the system to tag material for online retrieval – will access LCC online. For the foreseeable future, however, heavy reliance will still be placed on the print product, particularly among users outside the Library of Congress.

3 However, as conversion has progressed and individual schedules are merged into one database, consistency within individual schedules as well as across the scheme becomes ever more important. Increased consistency within and among schedules would have many advantages for proper use of the system and thus, in turn, for improvement in the quality of class-number assignment.

Recommendations for action

The recommendations set out here aim at achieving the following: providing for new topics; providing consistency in the treatment of common elements across the scheme; and balancing the need for logical arrangement with the integrity and stability of what now exists, both in current schedules and in new developments.

1 Develop overall editorial policies and guidelines for maintenance, revision, and new development of LCC; in this, consult both internal units and external bodies.

2 Define common elements that run through the entire scheme, such as format of captions, numbering of tables, style of notes, instructions relating to the use of tables, and cross-references among classes. Where feasible and without undue disruption of the existing collection, standardize the treatment of these common elements among related schedules and, if possible, across the entire scheme (see Williamson, 1995a).

3 Work toward systematizing the pattern of schedule revision, identifying needs, assessing available resources and personnel, and setting priorities. In recognition of the fact that libraries need time to absorb changes, pace the rate of thorough schedule revision, setting a maximum of, say, two or three a year. Place priority on future revisions and developments,

minimizing retrospective revision of existing schedules for the sake of local structuring.
4 Establish general guidelines for incorporating new topics, for pruning (see Williamson, 1995b, Recommendation, 5, 10, 11), and for standardizing both practice and terminology in respect to captions, instruction notes, cross references, and tables.

- *Re* new topics, consider expanding literary warrant to include not only LC's collection but also the collections of outside users; also develop and maintain models for new development (and for thorough revisions) for arrangement of common divisions (see Martel's seven points – Martel, 1911) and for the array of topical concepts.
- *Re* pruning, clean up the schedules, eliminating dual provisions, and consolidating or collapsing seldom used numbers (Morris, 1990).
- *Re* standardization, examine tables, captions, instruction notes, and cross-references; pay particular attention to terminology because that drives the individual schedule indexes on which a workable merged index to the whole system must be based.

5 Develop a policy on new developments: when they are warranted and justified, and where they should best be placed. If possible, avoid relocations that involve large blocks of existing topics, to minimize the need for reclassification.
6 Establish a research agenda, particularly on the question of LCC's potential as a retrieval tool; publicize it among the research community, and encourage and monitor-relevant research activities. Three particularly salient research questions in the years immediately ahead might be:

- Can the shelving and browsing/navigating functions of the Classification be effectively separated?
- Can expert systems be developed for manipulating tables and subarrangements? For synthesizing numbers?
- Can broad outlines of the schedules be effectively refined and expanded with a view toward their use as tools for online resources?

One suggested research question, on the possibility of creating a highly detailed broad outline of the Classification, could have great impact for those who are using LCC to organize Web resources. If the outcome were positive, the existence of such an outline would make it easy for managers of Web sites to tag material at a greater depth of analysis than is now the case. There should be few technical difficulties in developing such an outline; the major task would probably be dealing with variants and ambiguities in the terminology – perhaps by adding qualifiers and cross-references in some cases as a stopgap to thorough revamping caption terminology.

Another very promising area of research could be the question of separating the shelf location and browsing/searching function of classification. A cursory consideration suggests that even using multiple class numbers, given that it was kept clear that one was primary – in other words, a full call number and therefore the one to be used for shelving – would enhance browsing and searching considerably.

Currently, many of the recommendations and suggestions discussed above are in process of gradual implementation; some, particularly standardization or harmonizing of terminology throughout the schedules and the index, appear to be lower on the Library's priority list, no doubt because of other more pressing matters, especially the impending implementation of the new integrated system, Voyager.

References

Chan, Lois Mai (1995), 'Classification, present and future', *Cataloging and Classification Quarterly*, **21** (2), 5–17.
Classification Plus (1996 and 1995) *Cataloging Service Bulletin*, **71–74** (winter 1996), and **73** (50) (summer 1996).
Glassel, Aimee D. and Wells, Amy Tracy (1997), 'Scout Report Signpost: design and development for access to cataloged Internet resources', *Journal of Internet Cataloging*, **1** (3), 15–45.
Guenther, Rebecca S. (1996), 'Automating the Library of Congress Classification Scheme; implementation of the USMARC format for classification data', *Cataloging and Classification Quarterly*, **21** (3/4), 199–200.
LaMontagne, Leo E. (1961), *American Library Classification with Special Reference to the Library of Congress*, Hamden, CT: Shoe String Press, pp. 233–4.
Library of Congress (1991), *USMARC Format for Classification Data: including guidelines for content designation*, Washington, DC: Cataloging Distribution Service, Library of Congress.
Library of Congress, Bibliographic Enrichment Advisory Team (1997), Interim Report, for ALA 1997. Available at http://lcweb.loc.gov/catdir/beat/beat_ala97.html
Library of Congress, Office for Subject Cataloging Policy (1929), *Subject Cataloging Manual: classification*, Washington, DC: Cataloging Distribution Service, Library of Congress.
────── (1995), *Subject Cataloging Manual: shelflisting*, 2nd edn, Washington, DC: Library of Congress, Cataloging Policy and Support Office.
Martel, Charles (1911), 'Classification: a brief conspectus of present day library practice', *Library Journal*, **36**, 415; reprinted in Lois Mai Chan, Phyllis A. Richmond nd Elaine Svenonious (eds) (1985), *Theory of Subject Analysis: A Sourcebook*, Littleton, CO: Libraries Unlimited, p. 74.
────── (1929), 'The Library of Congress Classification: some considerations regarding the relation of book or library classification to the "order of the sciences",' in *Essays offered to Herbert Putnam by his Colleagues and Friends on his*

Thirtieth Anniversary as Librarian of Congress: 5 April 1929, New Haven, CT: Yale University Press, p. 327.

McKiernan, Gerry (n.d.), 'Beyond bookmarks: schemes for organising the Web', available at http://www.public.iastate.edu/~CYBERSTACKS/CTW.htm

McKiernan, Gerry (1997a), 'Handmade in Iowa: organising the Web along the Lincoln Highway', *D-Lib Magazine*, February.

McKiernan, Gerry (1997b), 'The new/old World Wide Web order: the application of "neo-conventional functionality" to facilitate access and use of a WWW database of science and technology Internet resources', *Journal of Internet Cataloging*, 1 (1), 48.

Morris, Leslie (1990), 'The frequency of use of Library of Congress Classification numbers and Dewey Decimal Classification numbers in the MARC file in the field of library science', *Technical Services Quarterly*, 8, 37–49.

Williamson, Nancy (1995a), *The Library of Congress Classification: a content analysis of the schedules in preparation for their conversion into machine-readable form*, with the assistance of Suliang Feng and Tracy Tennant. Washington, DC: Library of Congress, Cataloging Distribution Service. Recommendations #7, #7.3.4(a), #7.3.4(b)

—— (1995b), *The Library of Congress Classification: a content analysis of the schedules in preparation for their conversion into machine-readable form*, with the assistance of Suliang Feng and Tracy Tennant. Washington, DC: Library of Congress, Cataloging Distribution Service. Recommendations #5, #10, #11.

Appendix: Screen dumps from CyberStacks and Scout Report Signpost*

CyberStacks(sm) Main Main

Select A Subject Group

G	Geography, Anthropology and Recreation	
H	Social Sciences	
J	Political Science	
K	Law	
Q	Science	
R	Medicine	
S	Agriculture	
T	Technology	
U	Military Science	
V	Naval Science	

[CyberStacks(sm)](#)

* Reproduced by permission from CyberStacks and Internet Scout Project

Agriculture (S)

| Q-Science | R-Medicine | S-Agriculture | T-Technology | U-Military | V-Naval |

	Agriculture (General)	S
	Plant Culture	SB
	Forestry	SD
	Animal Culture	SF
	Aquaculture, Fisheries, & Angling	SH
	Hunting	SK

CyberStacks(sm)

Agriculture -- Forestry
(SD)

| Q-Science | R-Medicine | S-Agriculture | T-Technology | U-Military | V-Naval |

SELECT	SD
Forestry	1-390
Sylviculture	391-409.5
Conservation & Protection w/Forest Reserves	411-428
Exploitation & Utilization w/Timber Trees, Logging, Transportation, Valuation	430-557
Forest Policy & Administration	561-668
CyberStacks(sm)	SD

| S | SB | SD | SF | SH | SK |

Conservation & Protection w/Forest Reserves
(SD:411-428)

| Q--Science | R-Medicine | S-Agriculture | T-Technology | U-Military | V-Naval |

SD 411 Conservation and Protection. General Works

Forest Information

Summary:

Forestry Information is a database provided by the World Conservation Monitoring Center (WCMC) and its Forest Program Division. The database seeks to reflect "...holdings on forests, their diversity and conservation status worldwide...." Records are compiled from a variety of national and international sources; listings are provided only for those countries offered in the main menu selection.

Upon selecting a country from the title listing, the user will then have two information search options: (1) to view forest statistics; or (2) to view a map of the country's forests. Users who select the first option will find statistics on both forest cover and protected areas for their chosen country. Specifications concerning forest cover are subdivided within the records to reflect: forest and other wooded land, closed forest, natural forest, and the annual change of forest land. At the closing of the statistics is an area devoted to references for the sources of the data.

A selection of the map viewing option displays a full-color map of the country, noting forest coverage and protected areas. Included within the map is a mileage guide and a key to color codes used within the map.

The database is maintained by the World Conservation Center; Cambridge, United Kingdom.

To Search:

Select country of choice from main menu. Then select statistics display or map display.

SD 414.T76   Conservation and Protection. By Region or Country. Other Regions or Countries. Tropics

Tropical Forest Conservation and Development: A Bibliography

Summary:

    Tropical Forest Conservation and Development: A Bibliography "...pulls together, from various disciplines, literature relating to the conservation and sustained development of tropical forests. All of the publications cited are in the collection of the University of Minnesota Libraries and are available (photocopy or loan) from [the] Interlibrary Loan Division...." Upon accessing the bibliography's site, the user will find a Gopher menu offering three topics: (1) general information on the site; (2) browsing the site; and (3) searching the site.

    The first topic offers a general introduction, information on the site's creator, and contact information for copies of cited publications. The browse link produces the complete listing of all search topics: forest resources; deforestation; conservation and sustainable development; indigenous peoples; management, policy, and planning; trade and industrial development; nontimber forest products; research, education, and training; history; and bibliographies and general works. The search area offers a Gopher index search engine with a keyword field.

    To search the site, the user can activate the keyword field found under the "search" link or choose a topic from the "browse" link. In the case of the latter search method, users will find a list of titles displayed, presented in alphabetical order. Selecting a title then reveals its bibliographic entry. For books, the following is shown: author's name (last, first initial); year of publication; title of book; publisher (name and location); number of pages; description of contents; code number for site; and topic group of site. For articles, the following is found in an entry: author's name (last, first initial); year of publication; title of article; title of journal; volume, issue, and page numbers; description of contents; code number for site; and topic group of site.

    The site is maintained by Jean Albrecht; Forestry Library; College of Natural Resources; University of Minnesota; St. Paul, Minnesota.

To Search:

    Select "search link" and enter word into provided field. Or select "browse method" and choose topic of interest. Then select title of article to view bibliographic entry.

CyberStacks(sm)

The Future of Classification

The *Scout Report Signpost* contains only the best Internet resources, as chosen by the editorial staff of the *Scout Report*, cataloged and organized for efficient browsing and searching.

The Internet Scout Project, located in the Computer Sciences Department of the University of Wisconsin-Madison, is funded by the National Science Foundation. Its mission is to assist in the advancement of resource discovery on the Internet.

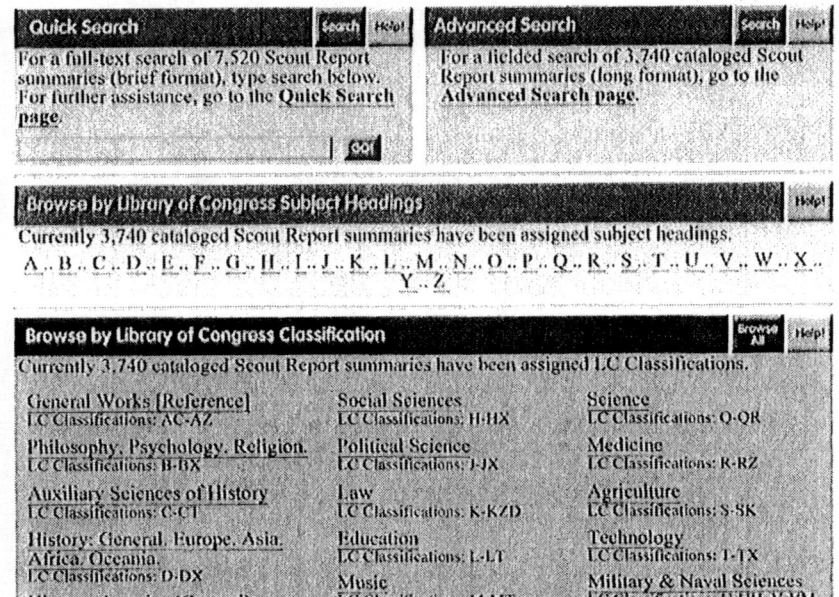

About Scout Report Signpost
Help!

Questionnaire

This site is best experienced with:

Netscape Navigator 3.0 or
Microsoft Internet Explorer

© 1999 *Internet Scout Project* Copyright Permissions

Comments, Suggestions, Feedback
Send email to signpost@cs.wisc.edu

Agriculture

LC Classification: S-SK

Browse by Library of Congress Classification

S - Agriculture (General)

SB - Plant Culture

SD - Forestry

SF - Animal Culture [Includes Veterinary Medicine]

SH - Aquaculture. Fisheries. Angling

SK - Hunting

All Agriculture (S-SK) Titles

[Home] [Quick Search] [Advanced Search] [Browse by Subject Headings] [Browse by LC Classification] [Help!]

© *1999 Internet Scout Project* Copyright Permissions

Comments, Suggestions, Feedback
Send email to signpost@cs.wisc.edu

SD - Forestry [6]

Displaying records **1-6** of **6** records found.
(6 records displayed)

Browse by Library of Congress Classification

1. **Neotropical Migratory Birds of the Kisatchie National Forest, Louisiana: Abstracts for Selected Species and Management Considerations** Signpost Full Description
   (http://www.srs.fs.fed.us/pubs/docs/gtr_so115.pdf)
   Some may find this June 1995 report by Robert Barry and others (.pdf format, 4257K) of interest; it reviews the scientific literature on thirteen species of Neotropical migratory songbirds breeding in the Kisatchie National Forest in Louisiana. Authors summarize "distribution, biology, habitats, and density" as well as population trends and...

2. **Proceedings of the XI World Forestry Congress** Signpost Full Description
   (http://www.fao.org/WAICENT/FAOINFO/FORESTRY/WFORCONG/PUBLI/DEFAULT.HTM)
   The United Nations Food and Agriculture Organization has recently made these two sites available. The first site, FAO Hypermedia Collections on Desertification, was created as part of the First Session of the Conference of the Parties (COP1) to the United Nations Convention to Combat Desertification (UNCCD), held in Rome, Italy...

3. **Satellite Observations of Forest Fires** Signpost Full Description
   (ftp://fermi.jhuapl.edu/www/seaspace/gallery/fire/fire.html)
   The Ocean Remote Sensing Group of the Johns Hopkins University Applied Physics Laboratory has made available a series of maps of some of the fifteen major wildfires that were burning Wednesday across 264,794 acres in six Western states--Oregon, California, Idaho, Wyoming, Utah, and Colorado. The images are not intended...

4. **Social Sciences in Forestry Bibliography: 1985-Present** Signpost Full Description
   (http://www-stp.lib.umn.edu/for/bib/SSiF.html)
   This quarterly bibliography, produced by the Forestry Library at the University of Minnesota, contains briefly annotated citations in 43 subjects in four major areas (forestry at large, forest management, forest goods and services, and forest industries). At present the bibliography contains over 30,000 citations, 1985 -present, which are available for...

5. **State of the World's Forests 1997** Signpost Full Description
   (http://www.fao.org/waicent/faoinfo/forestry/SOFOTOC.htm)
   The United Nations Food and Agriculture Organization provides this book (Adobe Acrobat [.pdf] format only), which "presents information on the current status of the world's forests, major developments over the reporting period (1995-1997), and recent trends and future directions in the

forestry sector." *SOFO* provides information on...

6. **Wild Land Fires Incident Management Situation Reports**   Signpost Full Description
   (http://vwww.vita.org/disaster/wildfire/)
   Volunteers in Technical Assistance (VITA), as part of its Disaster Information Service, is maintaining daily reports from the National Interagency Coordination Center (NICC) on U.S. wildfires. Each day the report details progress made in these fires, along with size, percent containment, estimated date of containment, and estimated losses and costs...

S-SK - Agriculture

[Home] [Quick Search] [Advanced Search] [Browse by Subject Headings] [Browse by LC Classification] [Help!]

© *1998 Internet Scout Project* Copyright Permissions

Comments, Suggestions, Feedback
Send email to signpost@cs.wisc.edu

10 Sources for investigating the development of bibliographical classification

M. P. Satija

Introduction

Sometimes described as an intellectual kingpin of our profession, library classification started to be seen as an area of academic studies only in the late nineteenth century. Quite aside from its practical day-to-day applications, the theory of the subject gradually began to attract international attention. S. R. Ranganathan wrote in the early 1950s that, by then, it had acquired all the features of a discipline (Ranganathan, 1951, p. 12). Furthermore, describing classification as a way of thinking systematically, he equated it with other highly developed academic disciplines such as mathematics, relating it to disciplines such as linguistics and philosophy (Ranganathan, 1962, p. 96). And, in 1975, another original thinker on the subject, Eric De Grolier, said that classification had come of age (De Grolier, 1975).

Naturally, praise for a subject from its practitioners can sometimes be excessive. Yet it may not be an exaggeration to say that the development and maturity of the library profession was accelerated by the application of modern classification methods to library management. Classification has exercised a marked influence on the course charted by the library and information profession and has been claimed as a foundation study therein (Foskett and Palmer, 1961). It is mostly for the influence of the Dewey Decimal Classification on library management that Melvil Dewey (1851–1931) is remembered as the father of the modern library profession. The subject has always attracted many of our best brains.

Classification fully displays the characteristic features and traits of a discipline. Its theory and practice are taught at the university level. It has a sound theoretical base and has drawn ideas from many subjects – including philosophy, psychology, taxonomy, epistemology, library user studies, linguistics, logic and mathematics (Dahlberg, 1985). Its practice is based upon a dynamic theory which is always in arrears of finding full practical applications. It has evolved its own terminology which is essential for learning and communicating its concepts, techniques and research. Individual and corporate research continues to take the subject forward. National and international conferences provide a forum for ideas and deliberations.

Thus there is now a large international body of literature. This paper seeks to be a personal selection and description of sources for investigating the evolution and potential further development of our subject.

Sources of history

While the origins of library classification can be traced to ancient times, its full history has not been written. To do so would be a most formidable and resource-intensive task. In Russia, a pioneering and commendable effort has been made: Shamurin, E. I. (1955) *History of Library–Bibliographical Classification*: Moscow: IzdatelÕstvo Vsesujsnoj Knizhnog Palaty. 2 volumes. (Title translated from Russian.) This monumental work begins with the classification system of the Assyrian King Assurbanipal (seventh century BC). The second volume, covering the nineteenth and twentieth centuries, ends with the Russian BBK (1965). It is a social history rather than simply a chronological one with a narrow perspective. A German translation of this work, by W. Hopp, was soon published and was reprinted in 1977. No other project of this magnitude and brilliance has been undertaken. One would wish to see it translated and updated in English.

Our subject's textbooks often shed light on its history, though the earlier works which they identify are often not bibliographical classifications as such. Two examples may suffice to illustrate this. A book by the American E. C. Richardson (1930) gives a list spanning the time from the ideas of Plato to the (then current) work of Bliss. The classic *Manual of Classification* (1994) has now been rewritten by Rita Marcella and Robert Newton. Both it and (especially) the older editions by Berwick Sayers and Arthur Maltby (1975) give space to the history of the subject, particularly its modern history.

The year 1976 was celebrated internationally as the Dewey Centennial. The event generated much literature, especially on the gradual development of decimal systems. Some specialist journals brought out issues dedicated to the occasion, for example *Herald of Library Science*. Many appropriate conferences took place. A bibliography of 135 monographs, sans annotations, on classification from 1876 to 1976 was compiled by Venkatappiah (1976). More modern lists of textbooks, with evaluative comment, have been compiled in the USA by Williamson (1994 and 1997).

The Centennial was clearly a good time to take stock generally of the course classification had traced and one stimulating, though brief, account is that of De Grolier (1976). For a conceptual history of library classification as an onward march from enumerative to faceted systems, Ranganathan provides the background from his own specific viewpoint (1965). For a full record of the conceptual history of classification, we await the completion of work by Francis Miksa of The University of Texas at Austin. Meanwhile, an article by him provides a useful short historical account (Miksa, 1993).

There are two collections of representative papers which are 'treasure troves' in their own right, but also serve as sterling sources for construing the history of classification thought. The first of these collections, by Chan et al. (1985), chronologically arranged, is an assembly of 32 classic writings of the period 1904–82. The authors are professional giants who have profoundly influenced the subject. This volume brings together the ground sources of the most basic and all-pervasive ideas 'for assessing the past and the present and illuminating the future'. It clearly depicts the genesis and development of modern ideas which made significant impact on the theory or practice of subject analysis and organization. The other collection, edited by Gilchrist (1997) reviews the progress made from the first International Study Conference on Classification Research (Dorking, 1957) until the seventh (London, 1997). This work divides into four sections, namely, the Dorking legacy; new tools; testing; questions and answers. Its 15 contributions include the reflections of some of the stalwart participants at Dorking and influential papers on information retrieval languages and practice.

Bibliographies

Research often begins with a bibliography and ends with a larger one! There are numerous classification bibliographies both general and special; exclusive and hidden; retrospective and current. A monumental and all-encompassing retrospective one in several volumes is that compiled by Ingetraut Dahlberg 1980–85: *International Classification and Indexing Bibliography*. Frankfurt am Main: Indeks Verlag (FID Publication 610). Sponsored by the German government and the FID/CR during 1980–83, this multi-volume work identifies, collates and lists literature of the previous thirty years. The result is a collection of about 20 000 references with abstracts, planned to be published to reflect a number of identified broad themes.

Only three of the planned five volumes have appeared. (Publication of the others is jeopardized by the retirement of Dr Dahlberg from active professional work.)

Arrangement is by a special system called Classification Literature Classification (CLC), a subsidiary of the International Coding Classification (ICC) which is explained both in the bibliography and in other writings by Dahlberg (1982). Entries provide full bibliographical details, and some are annotated. Each bears a serial number and class code. Each volume has author and subject indexes. Some knowledge of the classification in use is imperative for gainful browsing, although the indexes are adequate for the retrieval of entries. The entries themselves have been culled from varied and diverse sources – journal articles, reports, unpublished dissertations, books and chapters of books. The majority of references are in English, followed in descending order by Russian, German, French, other European, and some Asian languages. The work is without precedent and the largest bibliography ever compiled on any single aspect of our profession.

A less comprehensive general bibliography embracing both cataloguing and classification is that produced by Kapur (1988). It comprises 4510 highly select entries of the period 1951–86. About a third of these are on classification. The bibliography covers literature in English, wherever published, arranged within each part alphabetically by author.

We may choose too from numerous specialized bibliographies, both current and retrospective. The Dewey Decimal Classification is the subject of many bibliographies 'hidden' in journals or textbooks, but there is a distinct one by Gupta (1997), devoted to it. This gives details of 717 works in the English language with full details. It can also be accessed on the Internet at URL: http://www.oclc.org/oclc/fp/bibl/front.htm

For the Colon Classification there is a similar, but larger, work: this claims to be the largest bibliography on any single classification system. Compiled by Satija and Singh, it was published in 1994. It lists, in chronological order, 1350 references to a variety of documents, including unpublished dissertations originating in India or elsewhere. Every entry provides full bibliographical details. There are author and subject indexes.

Bibliographies of length devoted to other systems do not exist. But there are some on specialized aspects of our subject. In the 1960s, there was an acknowledged flight from DDC to the Library of Congress Classification. A bibliography on reclassification compiled then (McGaw, 1965) has just 39 references. Alas, as the matter of reclassifying is a recurring one, this bibliography may have some continued value in the context of present or future problems.

Studies of book numbers and author marks are re-emerging, and this is a fact that must be warmly welcomed. Some must have thought these an unworthy subject, for they received 'stepmotherly' treatment for a long time and there was certainly a need to redress the balance. They have a strong practical orientation, being indispensable for accurate shelf arrangement. Now, some expert systems are being designed to help apply Cuttermarks and other book numbers to create complete call numbers. There is an almost exhaustive bibliography on this topic of 181 items from 1878 to 1991, arranged chronologically with an author index. It was compiled by Satija and Comaromi (1992).

Further useful bibliographies include those by Stone (1993), Conway (1994) and Thomas (1995). Comment on the last of these may be useful since it is quite recent and concerns the new role of classification in the environment of electronic information. The entries cover books, articles and Internet resources on the role of classification within OPACs and information networks. Lengthy and clear abstracts enhance its value: it reads like a synopsis of current trends in classification.

Good textbooks on the subject, from several countries, should be easy to identify. Remember that they too all have useful 'concealed' retrospective bibliographies.

Current bibliographies

Literature on classification is regularly and adequately indexed in various services such as *Library & Information Science Abstracts*, London or *Information Science Abstracts*, New York. But current exclusive sources form the backbone of information sources for research and keep one posted on latest developments and research.

One such source, now edited by Gerhard Reisthuis, is: *Knowledge Classification Literature*: 1993– (formerly *Classification and Indexing Literature* 1974–). This is published as a regular section of the journal *Knowledge Organization*, and was established by Dahlberg. Every issue lists 300 to 500 references on broader areas of classification, indexing, subject analysis, concept theory and knowledge representation. It is organized by the Classification Literature Classification; outlines of this minute system are given at the beginning of every issue. The entire literature is surveyed under headings and subheadings. Every entry bears a class code and a four-digit serial number. The class number is accompanied by a language code in the case of non-English literature. Each entry provides full bibliographical details, and most are annotated. A computer-generated author index is provided. The range of literature is vast: drawn from many languages, it includes books, chapters, reviews and conference reports. The work is vital for current information on classification research and activity.

Some high-quality work is found in annual reviews. Two such are *The Year's Work in Subject Analysis*, as published for many years within Library

Resources and Technical Services, Chicago, and The American Society for Information Science publication available since 1996: *Annual Review of Information Science and Technology.*

The writings of a major innovator

In studying any subject, we must consider principal contributors as well as their publications. S. R. Ranganathan wrote on many aspects of librarianship, but was remarkably innovative in developing subject analysis, faceted classification, and a methodology for designing depth schedules. He was both prolific and ecumenical. Discovering new roles for classification along with many ingenious notational techniques, his influence was deep and decisive. One of the editors of this book (Maltby, 1998) describes him in our context as 'arguably, the greatest personality of the century... the influence of his ideas will stretch way beyond it'. Ranganathan's epoch-making work created a paradigm, winning the acclaim of his peers internationally. It may suffice to say that his testament on classification forms the bedrock on which much theory and practice stand today. His Colon Classification is supported by his various textbooks which, read carefully and in order, expound and enshrine those ideas which have had such deep and decisive influence. A noteworthy Festschrift was published in 1967. But, for the sake of brevity, only one later source of research about him, from the 1980s, is cited here (Satija, 1987). Nevertheless, the birth centenary in 1992, with IFLA holding a conference in New Delhi that year to mark the occasion, led to a spurt in Ranganathan studies. The wide range of material within these includes photographs and videofilm. Most of the more recent literature about him is either on his Five Laws or the classification writings.

Journals

As in all subjects, journals disseminate details of nascent research and their current issues inform us on the state of the art. Classification literature, sometimes very technical and jargon-ridden, is scattered through various journals. These include titles from various countries; four major ones are: *Library Resources and Technical Services, Journal of Documentation, International Cataloguing and Universal Bibliographic Control, Library Science with a Slant to Documentation and Information.*

But some extended comment is called for upon three which devote themselves exclusively to classificatory study.

First we should consider: *Knowledge Organization* 1974–. This, one of the most popular research journals, has a lively history. Started as *International Classification* by the enterprise of a group of German specialists led by Ingetraut Dahlberg, it was originally published half-yearly. Then, from 1980, when the publisher changed, it was issued thrice per year; from 1989 it became the quarterly organ of the International Society for Knowledge Organization, founded in 1989 with Dr Dahlberg as President. In 1993, the name was changed again to the present title. Though still an organ of ISKO, it now has another publisher and has Charles T. Gilreath as editor-in-chief. As a forum for discussion for all those concerned with wider areas of knowledge organization, it provides information on classification methods and processes by publishing original articles and reports on conferences, or ongoing research, along with detailed and scholarly book reviews. The issues taken up range from theoretical foundations to practical operations; from terminology to retrieval tools. A featured section on Current Knowledge Organization Literature has already been described. There are specialist contributors from many countries, and papers are generally refereed. Each issue has an editorial with comments on news and the current classification environment. There are so many features that it must be seen as essential for any student or teacher concerned with the international classification scene.

Another core journal is *Cataloging and Classification Quarterly (CCQ)*. This American publication has emerged as a journal of high standards, devoted to all aspects of bibliographical organization and subject analysis, with an expert editorial board. From time to time, special issues on a particular topic are published; occasionally an entire issue is devoted to the proceedings of a conference. The usual contents are long research and review articles providing an authentic mirror of current professional thinking. Book reviews appear as and when space permits. CCQ has now established a home page on the Internet to provide users with the table of contents, abstracts, editorial – and to call for papers. It is a hypertext destination for numerous other Web documents and also describes how to procure full-length articles from the Haworth Press, New York at URL: http://stirner.library.pitt.edv/haworth/ccq.html

A new quarterly from spring of 1997 comes from the same publishing house; one of its editors (Ruth C. Carter) is also editor of CCQ: *Journal of Internet Cataloguing: the international quarterly of digital organization, classification and access*. This promises to be a vital journal, aiming to inform professionals of research carried out in the electronic environment, particularly electronic materials available within the Internet. Its Web page is accessible at URL: http://www.jic.libraries.psu.edu

Current sources

The newsletters of classification organizations can be invaluable for keeping up to date. Frequently they are inserted in other publications. They include the *FID/CR newsletter* published in *Knowledge Organization*; and *Classification Issues for Knowledge Organization*, issued quarterly within the FID *News Bulletin*. The first of these has no rival in breadth of news coverage. The second is also excellent, although there is some natural emphasis on UDC activities therein.

The IFLA section on Classification and Indexing, established in 1981, publishes a newsletter as an annual loose-leaf brochure of a few mimeographed pages for circulation among its members and a few other interested professionals. This disseminates information on the section's activities, gives some attention to subject retrieval issues relating to the host country of the IFLA conference, and seeks to provide guidelines for subject authority files. It aims to provide a means for 'sharing different national experiences and of fostering an international perspective on classification and indexing'. An abbreviated version of this newsletter appears in *Knowledge Organization*. This journal also now carries brief summary proceedings of the work of The Classification Research Group in England. The journal publisher (ISKO) also disseminates therein its own news about the numerous international conferences it organizes.

It is important to have current information on developments within the individual classification schemes as provided via such publications as:

DC& (Decimal Classification: additions, notes and decisions)
Extensions and Corrections (to the UDC)
Library of Congress Classification Additions and Changes
Bliss Classification Bulletin (Fitzwilliam College Library, Cambridge, England)

The Library of Congress also publishes a *Cataloging Service Bulletin* and, available by subscription only, an electronic newsletter, *LC Cataloging Newsline*. There are also commercially published annuals which show accumulated changes to the Congress schedules.

Less well known internationally is the Russian BBK and the fact that it is kept updated by *Bulletin LBC*, Moscow, Russian State Library 1992–. This annual bulletin publishes news, along with details of extensions or changes. Only the first two issues are available in English (Sukiasyan, 1998).

Some other sources

Two very different but important issues concern the meanings of terms and the activities of people. Classification terms are explained in general professional glossaries and in some textbooks. The Dewey Decimal Classification gives guidance on its own existing and new terminology. The only dedicated specialist source as a glossary of all classification terms is a now quite outdated one published in India (Bureau of Indian Standards, 1964). Perhaps there is a vacuum here.

As for biographical information, the main specialist source remains a *Who's Who* edited by Dahlberg, published by FID in 1983. This gives biographical details and the major publications of about 700 professionals from 45 countries. The work is under active revision, and a new edition may be published by ISKO.

Sources on the Internet

This wonder lays open a vast ocean of information which can be brought from a great distance to one's elbow, as it were. Many classification organizations have created their home pages on the Internet. The scene is rapidly changing, but a good starting-point at present is a general database: *NetFirst*. Online it is accessible at URL: http://www.oclc.org/oclc/press/960219.htm This selective database and directory of sources available on the Internet was started early in 1996. Begun with 40 000 records and weekly updates, it strives to be current and comprehensive. Each record provides a full bibliographic description, with an abstract; Library of Congress subject headings; and DDC numbers.

A specialized source of advice for further Internet searching is that provided by Sha (1998). This links into a variety of sources including home pages, professional associations, national bibliographic utilities, cataloguing tools, and resources.

The Library of Congress home page is located at URL: http://www.lc web.loc.gov This home page allows searching of the Library computerized catalogue, the viewing of electronic exhibits and special collection details and the identification of publications and services. One may also search resources produced by the Library's Cataloguing Distribution Service.

Specialized libraries

Classification literature forms a sizeable collection in many institutions, but in international terms there are few remarkable specialized collections. Dr

Dahlberg maintained a large private library for many years which was accessible to scholars, but since her retirement the collection has been moved.

A specialized source worth mention is The Subject Analysis Systems Collection at The Faculty of Library and Information Science, University of Toronto, Canada. Its catalogue is accessible in the university's information system (UTLink) on the Internet. Because of this collection's coverage, which includes some adaptations and expansions of classification schemes, it is occasionally a unique source. Established in 1924, it has been at its present home since 1976, during which time it has been both pruned and augmented. The library offers a search and interlibrary loan service, for a fee, to all accredited researchers.

Conclusions

Although many aspects and publications have been mentioned, the restricted length of this chapter means there must be contractions and omissions. Bibliographical classification has come a long way from its first hesitant beginnings, and has still far to travel. Its literature is adequately covered by secondary information services, though primary sources have some gaps.

There is no full-length history of the subject compiled from primary sources. The history of the DDC is available, and that could be a model and inspiration for other systems to write their full histories (Comaromi, 1976). It was noted above that Miksa is working on a full new history of classification.

State-of-the-art surveys for classification are relatively few. It is hoped that the present volume will help fill that gap, but whenever we seek a concise account of current trends we still need to consult many sources.

Dahlberg's biographical work urgently needs to be updated. Current bibliographies are reasonably adequate, but there is an obvious void concerning the lack of an up-to-date specialist glossary of classification and indexing terms – though many are listed in more general sources. Doctoral and other dissertations in classification can be traced, though again only through checking out such general library and information sources as the work edited by Prytherch (1994). There is, in my view, a need for a classification handbook. Moreover, while there are sundry associations to promote research on aspects of classification, there is no clear centre to plan and execute research in all aspects of knowledge organization. If such a centre existed, it might well also become a depository and information clearing house within the context of the world's classification literature.

References

Bureau of Indian Standards (1964), *ISI Glossary of Classification Terms*, New Delhi: Indian Standards Institution.
Chan, L. M. et al. (eds) (1985), *Theory of Subject Analysis: a sourcebook*, Littleton, CO: Libraries Unlimited.
Comaromi, J. P. (1976), *The Eighteen Editions of the Dewey Decimal Classification*, Albany, NY: The Forest Press.
Conway, M. (1994), 'Research in cataloguing and classification . . . a selective annotated bibliography', *Cataloguing and Classification Quarterly*, **19** (1), 119–29.
Dahlberg, I. (1982), 'Information coding classification; principles structure and application possibilities', *International Classification*, **9** (2), 89–93.
—— (1985), 'Editorial', *International Classification*, **9** (2), 89–93.
De Grolier, E. (1975), 'A tribute to Dr Ranganathan', In: A. Neelameghan (ed.), *Ordering Systems for Global Information Networks*, Bangalore: FID/CR, 1979.
—— (1976), 'Classification one hundred years after Dewey', *Unesco Bulletin for Libraries*, **30** (6), Nov.–Dec., 320–26.
Foskett, D. J. and Palmer, B. I. (eds) (1961), *The Sayers Memorial Volume* London: The Library Association. (Palmer's personal contribution, pp. 202–12.)
Gilchrist, A. (ed.) (1997), *From classification to knowledge organisation: Dorking revisited, or, past is prelude*, The Hague (FID Occasional Paper 14).
Gupta, S. (1997) *Decimal Classification System: a bibliography for the period 1876–1994*, New Delhi: M D Publications.
Kapur, S. (1988), *Classification and Cataloguing; a select bibliography*, New Delhi: Harman Publishing House.
Maltby, A. (1975), *Sayers' Manual of Classification for Librarians*, 5th edn, London: André Deutsch.
—— (1998), Letter to the author, 15 June 1998.
Marcella, R. and Newton, R. (1994), *A New Manual of Classification*, London: Gower.
McGaw, H. F. (1965), 'Reclassification: a bibliography', *Library Resources and Technical Services*, **9**, 483–8.
Miksa, F. (1993), 'Classification', in Wiegard and Davis (eds), *Encyclopaedia of Library History*, Hamden, CT: Garland Publishing, pp. 144–53.
Prytherch, R. (1994). *Information Management and Library Science: a guide to the literature*, Aldershot, UK: Gower, pp. 92–4.
Ranganathan, S. R. (1951), *Philosophy of Library Classification*, Copenhagen: Ejan Munksgaard.
—— (1962), *Elements of Library Classification*, 3rd edn, Bombay: Asia Publishing House.
—— (1965), 'Library classification through a century', *Library Science with a Slant to Documentation*, **2** (1), March, 1–30.
Satija, M. P. (1987), 'Sources of research on Ranganathan', *International Library Review*, **19**, 311–20.
Satija, M. P. and Singh, A. (1994), *Bibliography of Colon Classification, 1930–1993*, New Delhi: M D Publications.
Satija, M. P. and Comaromi, J. P. (1992), Bibliography within their *Beyond Classification and Book Numbers*, New Delhi: Ess Ess, pp. 97–112.
Sayers, W. C. Berwick, (1926), *A Manual of Classification*, London: Grafton.
Sha, V. T. (1998), *Internet resources for cataloguing*, online at URL: http://www.law.missouri.edu./vianne/cat.htm

Stone, A. V. (1993), 'The elusive concept of aboutness', *Library Resources and Technical Services*, **37**, 277–98.

Sukiasyan, E. (1998), Letter No. 17/29 of 2 February 1998 to the author from Dr Eduard Sukiasyan of the Russian State Library.

Thomas, A. R. (1995), 'New roles for classification in libraries and information networks ...', *Cataloguing and Classification Quarterly*, **21** (2), 91–118.

Venkatappiah, V. (1976), 'Literature in library classification: a select bibliography of books published during the last hundred years', *Herald of Library Science*, **15** (3–4), July–Oct., 218–24.

Williamson, Nancy J. (1994), 'Subject analysis systems', in P. Johnson (ed.), *Guide to Technical Services Resources*, Chicago: American Library Association, pp. 68–85.

────── (1997), 'Subject analysis systems', in P. Johnson (ed.), *New Directions in Technical Services; trends and sources 1993–1995*, Chicago: American Library Association, pp. 86–118.

Index

Argus Clearing House 51–2
Aristotle 34, 36–7
Association for Computing Machinery Classification 63
Automatic classification and indexing 12, 52–4, 63–4

BBK Classification (Russia) 136
Beall, J. 86
Bell, B. L. 88
Bibliographic Classification (BC) xi, 71, 74, 77, 78, 99, 136
Bibliographical aids, complementary to classification 22
Bliss, H. E. 71
Bliss Classification Association 99
Boolean logic, used for searching 9–11, 39, 52, 60
Broad subject arrangement 4
Broad System of Ordering 72, 77, 78
Brown's Subject Classification 77
BUBL Information Service 61–2
Burton, P. 9

Carter, R. C. 135
Catalogues 2–3, 5–7, 26–7
  of Internet resources 61–2
CATRIONA project 47
Chain indexing 77
Chan, L. M. 87, 111, 115, 131
Citation indexing 64
Citation order 74–5, 79, 83, 87
Classification
  in alphabetical catalogues 7–8
  arguments against it 9, 26, 28
  as a tool to stimulate exploratory searching 27, 37–8
  attitude to it in the United States of America 7
  automatic 12, 53–4, 62–4
  in bibliographies and reference works 22
  dangers of ignoring its principles xiv, 16, 20, 43, 54, 79
  essential in everyday life 2–3
  grows into a distinct discipline 129–30
  history and literature reviewed 132–7
  in on-line retrieval 43–55, 65–6
  journals on 134–5
  multi-dimensional 65
  place in professional information science curriculum xii, 9, 21
  potential discriminatory power 36, 37–8
  problems and limitations 24–8, 65–6, 70
  as a saver of time 19
  should be in school curriculum 16
  still essential for information management 15–16, 30
  as a 'switching language' 29, 79, 88
  for Web resources 46–8, 54
'Classification Plus' (LCC) 44, 107
Classification Research Group (UK) 16, 69, 71, 136

Clifton, H. O. and Sutcliffe, A. G. 14
Coates, E. J. 70
Cochrane, P. and Johnson, E. 90
Cockshutt, M. 86
Colon Classification (CC) 70, 73–4, 78, 134
Computer technology
    offers flexibility for catalogues 5–7, 26
    offers new dimension for classification 26, 66–7, 76, 78–9
    possible unconscious abuse of it 20
    see also Internet, World Wide Web
Cooperation between classification schemes xiv, 27, 90, 100, 102, 106
Costs 24, 30, 51, 75
Courtenay, C. 1
Cutter Tables 86, 132–3
Cyber Dewey 47
Cyberstacks 46, 48, 61, 111–12, 120–27

Dahlberg, I. 131, 135, 137, 138
Dawkins, R. 25
De Bono, E. 70
De Grolier, E. 129, 131
DESIRE Project 46
Dewey, M. 28, 69, 74, 129
Dewey Decimal Classification (DDC) 47, 62, 78, 81–90, 132
    complementary to UDC 96
    embryonic faceted classification in early editions 69
    meaningful notation in DDC 87
    reasons for popularity 88–9
    revision and relocation of classes 78, 83–5, 136
    worldwide use 88–9
Dewey for Windows 44, 78, 81, 83, 84, 85–6, 89
Dickens, C. 37
Dickens House Classification 71
Directory of Networked Resources 47
Dodd, D. G. 12
Domain Name Server System 64
Dublin Core 61
Dykstra, M. 9

Edinburgh Engineering Virtual Library 63
Electronic resources, classification of 45–8

Electronic versions of classification schemes 44, 78, 81, 85–6, 94, 106–7
Ellis, D. 53
Emerging subjects 85
ERIC database 75
Excite (Search engine) 12–13

Faceted classification xiii, 14, 22–3, 69–79, 87
Fem/DDC 89
Ford, H. 1–3
Foskett, A. C. xiii
Foskett, D. J. 22, 71, 75
Freeman, R. R. xi
Full text databases 9

Gilchrist, A. 20–1, 93, 131
Glassel, A. D. and Wells, A. T. 112
Godby, C. J. 90
'Grey material' xii, 46
Guenther, R. S. 109–10
Guiding 73
Gupta, S. 132

Hellman, L. 28
Hildreth, C. R. 11
Huestis, J. 7
Hunter, E. J. xii

Indexes to classification schedules 15, 76–7
    meaningful retrieval via index 87
    revision of index in LCC 110–11
Information retrieval systems
    theory and practice should agree 38–40
Information skills 16
Integrative level theory 71
Integrity of numbers 75, 114
Internet 12, 21, 46, 59–67, 90, 111–12, 137
    see also World Wide Web
Iyer, H. and Giguere, M. 89

Jevons, W. S. 25
John Moores University, Liverpool 6
Johns, C. 45, 55
Jones, N. 12
Jul, E. 46

Kapur, S. 132
Keywords 21, 44

Koh, G. S. 44–5
Kowalk, W. 50

Lesk, M. 45
Library of Congress Classification (LCC), xiv, 48, 62, 78, 105–18
   flexibility of 113–15
   index 110–11
   and the Internet 111–12
   revision and relocation of classes 107–11
Library of Congress Subject Headings 9, 62, 70, 84, 85, 90, 107, 108
Limitations and problems in classification see Classification
Line, M. 76
Liu, S. 54, 87
Lloyd, G. A. xi, 93, 98
Lynch, C. 59

McIlwaine, I. xiv, 90, 96
McKiernan, G. xiv, 46, 48, 61, 111–12
Maltby, A. 1, 4, 134
Marc records 77–8
Martel, C. 108, 113, 117
Measures in information retrieval see Recall
Medicine, classification of 63, 99
Metadata 61
Miksa, F. 52, 131, 138
Mills, J. xi, 77, 96
Mitchell, J. S. 49
Morris, L. 117
Mundie, D. 47

Neuminster, S. M. 51
New, G. R. 83
Norman, B. 1
Notation 13–15, 72–6
   meaningful notation in DDC 87, 90
   retroactive 74, 87
   seminal mnemonics 70

OCLC Forest Press 62, 78, 82, 88, 97
Octave Device 73
Olson, H. A. and Ward, D. B. 89
On-Line Public Access Catalogue (OPAC) 5–7, 50
Organization and management of schemes 77–9

see also under names of individual schemes

Precis system 76
Principle of inversion 74

Quasi-publications xii
Quinn, B. 7, 16

Ranganathan, S. R. xi, 23, 51, 67, 69, 70, 73, 129, 134,
Reader interest categories 4
Recall and relevance measures 20, 33–5, 39, 61, 64
Reclassification 75, 132
Relevance measures see Recall
Research activities 23, 39–40, 117–18, 131
   in DDC 90
Revision and relocation of classes
   in DDC 78, 83–5, 136
   in LCC 78, 107–11, 114, 136
   in UDC 75–6, 78, 95, 97–100, 102, 136
ROADS project 47
Russell, B. 26–7

Satija, M. P. 78, 132, 133
Schneiderman, R. A. 11, 16
Scorpion project 53, 63–4, 90
Scott, N. and Basu, A. 16
Scout Project 48, 111–12
Search engines 9, 12–13, 45, 60–61
   see also Excite, Yahoo!
Search strategies 27
Sellars, R. 3
Sha, V. T. 137
Shafer, K. 64, 90
Shakespeare, W. 33
Shamurin, E. I. 130
Short, N. 20
Social Sciences Information Gateway 47
Special classifications 44, 63
Svenonius, E. 50, 88
Swank, R. 21–2
Swanson, D. R. 41
Switching languages see Classification

Taylor, G. 14
Thesauri 8–9, 76, 89
Thomas, A. 133

Trotter, R. 44
Truncation 15
Twain, M. 36

United Kingdom Office of Library
  Networking 65
United States MARC format 89
Universal Decimal Classification (UDC)
  47, 66, 72, 75–6, 93–103
  compared with DDC 96–7
  Master Reference File 94
  revision and relocation of classes 78,
    95, 97–100, 136

van der Walt 46–7
Venkatappiah, V. 130
Vico, G. 34, 37, 38

VINITI 94
Virtual Libraries xi, 30, 44, 49–50, 63, 65
Vizine-Goetz, D. 49, 62, 90
Voyager System 106, 118

WAIS/World Wide Web Project 47, 66
Warner, J. xii–xiii
Wellisch, H. 52
Will, L. 44
Williamson, N. J. 99, 116–17, 131
Woodward, J. 49, 51
World catalogue (WorldCat) 85
World Wide Web 12, 47–8, 61, 64, 66–7,
  103, 117
  see also Internet

Yahoo! Inc. 12, 45, 55, 63